This Void Beckons

a Cracked Jar Press collection

Also from a.j.k. o'donnell

Nicoteane and Other Foolish Mistakes

This

Void

Beckons

a.j.k. o'donnell

This Void Beckons
Edition: 1st

ISBN 978 0 9977670 0 1

Library of Congress Control Number: 2016911378

Printed and bound
in the United States of America
Paperback Edition 2018

To schedule a speaking engagement with a Cracked Jar Press author
or to inquire about orders of works, please contact our
Relations Department: executiverelations@crackedjarpress.com

Cracked Jar Press is an independent publishing house that seeks to produce
works of literature with implications far greater than storytelling.
These works seep into the fabric of the human experience
and forever mark their place.

Cracked Jar Press
United States of America
www.crackedjarpress.com

for you

dearest companion

as a member of our collective human ancestory

5. 31. 16.

Perhaps there is but only one true sin.

To deny oneself from knowing

the individual who occupies their mind.

The Pathway

A Forewarning;

There is still time to euthanize this covenant.

Give its pages, thick with unpredictability, back to the bookseller. You may depart from your path before you have reached its virgin crossroads.
This binding is neither a prerequisite for entry to
heaven nor hell, contingent upon your respective prospection.
You may abandon this readership unscathed.

However, I implore you to consider those who have walked this road before you. History and holy books alike, which are merely one and the same, call them the enlightened ones. The martyrs. The saviors. The peacemakers.
The demigods.
The gods themselves.

Divine understanding comes at a price
you must be willing to indulge.
You can spare yourself the journey, but do not expect to find a way to discovery or rebirth.
There is but one road and it beckons now.

This expedition has been given many names.
Calvary. Hijrah. The Middle Way.
The Paths to Liberation. Exodus. Faith. Morality.
Modern science calls this ancient walkway the nervous system: axons, synapses, the very interweavings of the human mind.

This is your enlightenment.
Your crucifixion.
Your sacrifice of sacred cleansing.
The acquiring of deific wisdom.

Yet, this is not hell you see.
This odyssey leads anywhere but.

Hell is a concept here.
A choice.
As is heaven.

A choice which you dictate within these pages.

We are merely the curators of this primordial voyage.
Whilst you, if content in proceeding, are the willing participant.

Choose.

It Beckons

there is a silence here
a hollow presence

no
this is not slumber
nor is it the grasp of death

this

this is the Void

it calls to you softly now
bids you welcome
with melancholy majesty
intimacy of memories
hidden long ago
with patience only a child knows

it is daunting
engulfs your breath
thick like aged molasses
cooing you forward

drumbeats echo
dirt rustles
the breeze above
hushes

now

fall

fall

into the Void

begin

again

....

as you fell
you said you felt

nothing

lacking of life cues
separation of mind from senses
such is the wonderment of this primitive place

existence and erasure
consummate

a tangible

catastrophe of confusion

yet

beauty mingles

for here
is the very birthplace of humanity

cosmic rhythm
ancient choral melody

lingering quaver
pulsating in a most gorgeous spiraling continuum
uncontained
yet measurable
left to outlast time itself

clearly
all this space lacks is illumination

pathways forward
unlit
remaining stationary
in apprehension on how to produce a light source

look inward
dearest one
there within your pocket
a meager box
beneath the fold
rows of matches
strike one

give the flame life
herald your presence to this hallowed site
with triumphant might
humble gift
prayer of wick and wood

retrieving a simple stick
you spend a moment studying the shape
how intriguing
an object so small
capable of such destruction
as with a human heart
power can be found in the most unlikely of places

with that contemplation
you make your choice

by friction movement
phosphorous chorus
infernos cascade
twirling through the air
expose a most stunning surrounding

Cremations

upon witness

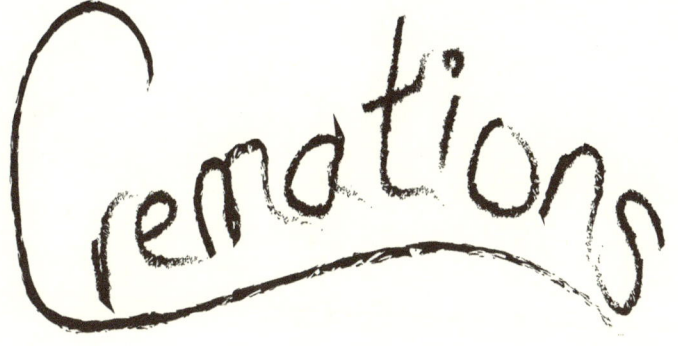

one may learn

consecrated annihilation

such a sight

blazes which do not burn
will not lick lips
or scorch tongues

heat is present
yet
destructive qualities of this ancient element
can not be felt

flames dance into breezes
hurricanes of awing radiance
spiral towards ceilings
floors
walls
like an overturned canister of melted copper
slivering throughout the cavern

majestic slowness
but timeless flow
fire spills into every crack of this ancient place
each direction overflows with unending brilliance
as though a bold sculptor
had fashioned every space a halo of lustrous magnitude

observe

illumination of the Void

your journey ahead

commences

roaming the ruins

definitions of worth
deem such sights before you
obsolete

soil
parched
peelable as the flesh of a seared forearm

once the focal point
of your world
now folds into destructive decay

gaze around
relish in what the blaze shows you
these are your memories
your ruins

enveloped by cover of cicada melodies
fading flicker of a solitary lamppost
eroded
familiar concrete
paves the street before you

homes adorned in vibrant hues
synthetic chandelier light penetrates upon fresh lawns
symmetrically reflected
either side of this road
identical
constructed upon prosperity
security
ethically labored valor

molding
partially consumed
cigarettes lay scattered
in curb corners
cracks curling up edges of weary concrete

into focus
far edge of this avenue
a dimly lit structure
quietly nestled among these grand buildings
reminiscent of your birth home
offsetting

halting at yard end
you gaze upon the shape still standing
many memories
transpired within those walls

lumber frame
painted shades of forgotten grief
sidewalk splattered by scraped knee calamities
bare foot worn grass

temple to a distant time
fading into shadows of another presence
fresh owners
carve new memories into floorboards
once walked in sleep wear
by young soles

from darkening streets
mechanical wailing swells
breaking your fixation
with indistinguible momentum
a vehicle scuttles past
accompanied by chilly gusts

come
there is more to behold

ushered by city glowings
pavements curve toward a quiet coffeehouse
fragmented neon sign crackles
displays a misspelled messsage

afterhours
doors bolted
frost stained window panes
expose a vacant interior

overturned wooden chairs
meticulously stacked upon tabletops
recently scrubbed demitasses
gently catalogued by color
rest on a sunken countertop
prepared for serving when morn arrives

surely a delightful venue
one you have entered before
no doubt
engaged in conversations of the soul
wrote critical disquisitions
studied those who occupied
now empty seats

recognize the significance
this place holds to you
every experience which transpired within
whether admirable or shameful
notions learned
projects conceived
honor the parts of you left here

for you must bid adieu
extensive path onward
does not conclude here

constructed slopes
converge with climbing road
steering you upward
elevated trek
lining the avenue
familiar buildings lay in dismay
crumbling beneath the weight of time

marketplace
where guardians purchased nutrition
staples for adolescent consumption

bookshop
concaving roof
mismatched
missing shingles
adorn a haven you once visited
leaving your world behind
in pursuit of more fascinating universes

institution of academic propriety
where textbooks gave way to doubts
formation of personal ideologies
defiled by ones who degraded you
never gazed into your soul
merely exterior preordination
without regard to internal conviction

each place you have marked
by previous breaths
sinking into ruinous resplendence
headstones to buried past
fashioned by what some call choices
others title happenstance

regardless
these are your ruins
tombs of a bygone presence
relics left behind
appointed no stewards
subjected to cognitive disownment

reaching gradient crest
your pathway peculiarly obstructed
iron rods collectively aligned
connecting to form a corroding gate
positioned at plinth of a duplicate slope

contained within metal partitions
a most primeval practice
supplying earth below
those who relied upon its fruits

bestrewn atop muddy surfaces
monuments to those departed
lingering legacies
narratives etched into granite

traveling further into the necropolis
structures become distinguishable
mausoleums without placards
boulders lacking monikers

until a simple stone
delicately inscribed
a name that you know
this person you remember
passing premature
leaving before you were prepared
crevice never replenished
a sorrow you will always hold

through the solace of silence
this place emits
a soft wail wafts into the air

ahead
descending upon origination site
behind cover of meager shrubs
a figure trembles before an unmarked grave
recently plowed
imaginably
enshrouding something which has passed
to a resting place
within and of
the earth

a child
at the base
of the mound

diminutive hands
contrast the broad shovel they enclose
weeping at the root of the mammoth incline
a small child kneels

do you recognize their features
curvature of their spine
the way their young hair dangles
pigment of their illuminated flesh
this child
once was you

why were they left here
cast aside before the fruition of growth
this body
has never known the malice of maturation
shedding of childhood
loss of supernatural knowledge

why are they locked here

will they ever forget

will they ever remember

such pain from the onset
comfort stripped

left in cathedrals of uncertainty
poised to pray for a sunrise
one which shall never come

now
this child sits
lathered in dirt
decaying soil
whimpering

for a loss
they do not comprehend

beside them
a wooden casket
rests in fresh mud
pulled from the earth by a large shovel
guided with young hands
prepared for burial

beneath fastened lid of mahogany
one would find a heartbreaking
collection of corpses

letters never received
photographs of people
long ago forgotten

first pebbles skipped across fluid silky surfaces
first pebble
to fall beneath the waves

each dandelion petal

copper coin
hollow star
which did not return with wishes granted

a blanket
torn with age
cuddled by an innocent
who believed the world would be gracious
colors dimming from dyed weavings

tear stains
one from the first time
they gazed upon a deer mangled on pavement
one from the last time
they recognized their father's fading scent
one from a time which may never come
moment of pure liberation
finding solidarity in another

finally
a sealed envelope
without postage or designation
guarding a prayer once spoken
transcribed grievance
to a god
who never received enclosed contents

certainly
this child is hurting
yearning for closure
unconditional love

speak to them
provide comfort
indulge their sadness
for you once knew the security of innocence
and how hastily it ceases

approaching the child
your presence remains unacknowledged

despite placing your hand
onto their fragile shoulder
still
no response transpires

perhaps now is not the time
for this child to know comfort
perchance
one day
they will greet the one
whom they have longed for

come
your path yonder
reaches much farther than this child

ascend this mound
atop
an ancient construction
one which has morphed with each builder
nevertheless
always employed to congregate faithfuls
beneath common understandings

they have obtained deific communication
any others who claim
are heathens

yet heathens shall say the same

in the end
one is left with nothing more
than a universe of heathens
divided
conflicted

a man abandoned in the sanctuary

erect above
grimly resolute
a steeple crowns the structure before you
bathed in hues of hypocrisy
haven to righteousness
epicenter of religious folly

crumbling
man-made canons
seep out of shattered glass windows
hymns to a holy one
polluted with pseudo-altruistic preachings
birthright of the chosen
disgrace to saviors
pure prophet disregarded
erased from walls

you must enter

steps beneath
cracking from weight of misusage
scattered without method
poorly aligned for procession
sink into soil below
do not linger on the stones
stationary surely means eventual submersion

reaching summit
mighty doors firmly contain inner worlds
unscathed by abominations
secular worlds undoubtedly impose
centered iron handles
adorned in majestic oxidation
dare you to engage
placate their desire to be used once more

you must open these oaken magistrates

auguring your intrusion
screeching echos
berate your body
reverberating throughout the grand atrium

deflating to ease
silence manifests
a novel
yet seemingly aged
vibration
surely no one is worshiping at this hour

proceeding into the holy dwelling
sounds swell
startling shrieks pierce into the ceiling

do not move
stand here
only peer onwards

ahead
near the base of the first prayer bench
amidst sacred shadows
a silhouette

a man
holds an object
as one cradles the putrefying limbs of a plague-devoured child
with deep heartache and terrified caution

closer examination
exposes the shape as a binding of papers
the man is shouting
pleading
plucking pages from this ancient text
showering the ground with a rain of consecrated scribbles
fluttering to the floor

delicate as shedding feathers of a mockingbird
each pulled sheet consummates twins
duplicated births from the binding
deny this man
relief he seeks

whatever could he be searching for

a passage of such importance
constituting a cursed crusade of eternal servitude
slave to miscalculation

your internal inquiries are interrupted
for now
with magnificent velocity
chilling magnitude
directed to deity above
he speaks

where

where is it written

which was my blunder
hymn falsified
prayer tainted with unholy hands

where did I cease to follow you
dedication to your dogma
lifetime of praise
divine discretion perpetually painted on my lips

quivering with exasperation
the man forcefully releases the book onto the tile
thudding
as does a heavy heart
casting himself alongside the discarded volume
pounding upon granite surfaces

perhaps now
his deity is below

why can I not hear you
see your face
feel your touch

I prayed
worshiped
performed as your holy book directed
condemned those who violated your will
campaigned for your pureness
yet
now
there is nothing

nothi

nnn

each proclamation
pounding of fist
pleadings exude into the floor
inaudible
unheard
forsaken

come
leave this man
for the sake of his dignity
forever searching in empty places
such is the burden of the righteous ones

gazing around
hoisted into the ribs of this stone structure
panes imbued with subtle grandeur
stain the air with shades
palates would envy

approach the window there
what do you see
out over the vale

a great source of purified water
river within the Void
unrestricted
absorbing into jaws of unseen canals
corners
descents

upon crystal movement
a small ship catches a tremendous gust
gliding without grace of form onward

no
that is not a vessel of planked variety
a figure once more
woman perhaps
running
sprinting on the water
curious you must be

there
beside the window
a door
how fitting
unseen departure
from a place to revel in iconic facades

marvel closer
at this miraculous allusion

a woman walking on the water

take caution
stones can be unforgiving unto bare feet

with no distinct pathway
clearly this slope is not frequently ventured

dry crags
creases of clay and dirt
incongruous patches
occasional viridescent fingers
gnawing for sunlight
sunken below sod
prickle skin an irritated indigo

arriving upon sand-coated banks
you pause
the women
now within audible radius
unmistakingly sobbing
howling with an agony
horrifying to merely fathom

one she unconditionally cherished
submerged
below ravenous currents

believing the unobtainable can be procured
if only one does not cease seeking
whomever she is searching for
can not be revived

who could the departed be
to decree such desperate denial
a child perhaps

drifting down to depths of decomposition
flesh extracted from unrelenting womb
stillborn sorrow
never able to show them the stars
teach them familial heritage
whisper them lullabies
see them age

or infant born
but with fixed expiration
left to live for only moments
before returning to a soothing sanctuary
separation of spirits
mortal divider
confinement to a most horrid loneliness

an adolescent
terrible misfortunes
irrevocable tragedy
juvenile folly

to look upon your silent child
kiss them goodnight
one final time
before an eternal slumber
washes them away

possibly a parent

offspring rearer
ones who impart
inherited wisdom
chromosomal chorus embedded within you
a painful sound
when instruments go dark
section of the orchestra omitted
part played
nevermore to emit their vibrations

nay

dear comrade
one who shared years of laughter
intimate moonlit conversations
quieted fears
comforted dolours
now decaying body
memories corroding
unrelinquished
nonetheless diminishing

question no longer dear one
settling sobs
morph into words
as the woman laments

what more could I have done

was their clock decided upon
long before I knew their name
touched their face
held their frame in my own

why was I the one left
cursed to carry memories
unaccompanied in this hollow place
unfulfilled fruition

where is the justice
mercy
promise of joy for the burdened
how can I reclaim a soul
swallowed by time

was life
not a gift they were meant to bear

was their demise
work of my own hands
by my fault
were they taken

I was not there
not present at the moment they left
I only seek one last embrace
to know this is the end
before it is so

grant me a single sentence
to tell them once more
how much they mean to my soul
how broken I have become
how much I yearn for their heartbeat to resound
through the stillness that comes at night

I only ask
for a simple goodbye
which would seal the gape I can not fill

please
if anyone can hear my cries
breathe life back into that which has been forsaken

oh
dear one
why do you weep for her

you must know of this heartache

her burden is not foreign to your own soul
loss of one most valued
taken by the apathy of time
perhaps you may offer her solace

beginning to approach her
your plan is delayed

for frightened
as if a stalking predator
suddenly sensed
danger closing in

the woman rapidly charges across the water
horror dripping down her cheekbones

mirroring her pace on land
you sprint parallel

her view pointed down
following the movement
of an object below

abruptly she halts
object below appears to have caught itself
in a patch of reeds

seizing her opportunity
the woman reaches into her clothes
retrieving a collection of rope
fashioned as a thin net

uncoordinated yanking
snags rope between pocket lining
and hands forcing hastily

frayed material gives
ripping a cry of agony unto itself
leaves a large hole in its wake
noticing the sudden decrease in effective usage
the woman panics
tugging with considerable force
once more

only to tear her means of rescue further

a final wrench
pulls remaining rope
out into unrestricted space

distressed she locates the damage
finding a hole to broad
for any object to hold
rendered useless
by her own hand
the woman has destroyed her last resource

confronting her predicament
hopelessness before her
she howls

no
no
please I beg of you
no

dropping to her knees
she claws without fruition
attempting to burrow through the surface
splitting bones
cracking skin
her fingers ooze blood
as water rushes
relentless in denying her entry

hoping you may aid her
you step forward from where you have stood
once at genesis of shoreline
you gaze upon the one she desires to save
just below surface level
floats a most disturbing sight

a body
water-torn
deteriorating skin
rotted open
crusting eyelids
expose hollowness manifest
nothing

face disfigured
frame wilting
dissolving into an echo
merely a vessel of what was once flesh

treading forward
your footing sinks into the river
astonished to find the water to be liquid
you close in on the pair
only to be struck by unseen currents
heaving you underneath

sputtering
you choke for air
tides deny your request
entrenching you deeper under careening movement
do not panic
conserve what oxygen you can collect

short-lived moments above surface level
gift you breath
in the distance a figure
rushes after an unoccupied body

bidding her well
you gulp one last helping
before being submerged once more
twisting
rushing
directionless darkness
you sweep on downstream
unsure of when waves will wane

a cloth worn by time

fear not
your plunge into the undertow
now subsides
currents propel you toward shore ahead
with a kiss onto sand
waves lick barren dirt
you are still

rest
here
upon coarse
infertile ground

afar
into the treeline
growth is evident
here this is not so

disrupter of germination below
becomes evident when gazing up

a textile
suspended above
separates sea from soil
diffuses light from touching beneath its shadow
marker of entrance to woods beyond
graceful guardian
specter of serenity

you may approach
peer upon glyphics
which seem to dance
in between translucent weavings

but
be warned
this beauty is not one of benevolence

behold
the tapestry of human existence

bodies are burning
stripped bare

a child
with the nose of your grandmother
she is bleeding
begging
a man
bruises her with a broken bottle

a soldier
face down
body
peeled open by metal and powder
left to rot
in the name of patriotism

tied women
stewards of Volta surge
cuffed by shackles of imperialism
bartered for coins
bodies entered unconsented
bent spines
sun-gnawed flesh
harvest fields in foreign lands

villages
burning
children running
reaching for their sisters
men atop stallions
torches thrown into canvass lodgings
tribal drumbeats fading
peaceful
sacred lands
industrialized

young boy
sweet child
venturing an empty road
imagining possibilities his future holds
walking home
soul stolen by steel
for a skin he did not choose
scarlet-stained sidewalk
water and soap
wash away atrocities

the face of a man
head adorned in spikes
whittled from a plant
lovers desire
weeping for the world
cheekbones sunken inward
legs prepared to succumb
thanks the woman before him
his Void had beckoned

a mother
beats a little boy
pinned limbs restrain
clumps of thinning hair
extracted from smooth scalp
blood caked fingernails
wiped onto fresh carpet

tomorrow
children will laugh
call the boy stupid
faggot

carbon monoxide
rain of onyx flames
engulf beings
locked in concrete cages
bodies disintegrating
women snap infant necks
saving children from the painful death
breathing had become

naked women
twine necklaces
enlarge pupils
dye necks violet
witchcraft is their legacy
innocence unconsidered
fair trial denied

children of Abraham
slaughter siblings
in the name of their mother
peace is never one sided

the girl wanted violation
a man yells
he will pick up roadway trash
once a week
she will die from childbirth complications

a woman
born with miscommunicated alignment
body she could not fully call home
stabbed in the chest
breasts pulled from her ribs
as though womanhood
hinges on physical constructs

explosions
people are praying
gunshots
people are mourning
babies are falling

churches
burning
men hanging from trees
hate splattered on pulpits
severed heads lay on beaches

a young girl
mutilated
stoned
unworthy

suits sip scotch
make deals
pollute waterways
indigenous worlds drink

nurturer
in anguish
the lifeless child in her hands
moments before
below her heart

death rows
serenades of innocence
ignored by government quotas

splintered skulls
drip blood
generations before labored to create

a sparrow
flutters above a decaying city
residents left to starve
humans have become disposable

in the distance
a sole echo
solemnly cries
tells of a troubled past
seemingly hopeless future
for the cloth continues to unfold
eternally depicting
the story of humankind

a beast of great brutality

human will can be

there is no peace here
time has only quickened
nothing has changed

as long as humankind
believes they can harness the will of gods
moralities become mythologies
destruction reigns
definition of dignity

rewritten

agony covered in ivy

open your eyelids love

your ankles twisted down
you must have fainted

the cloth is painful to bear witness
history is hard to comprehend
yet
many deny the cloth exists

our world is unblemished
they say
mention wars in history books
lenses capture victories of expanding nations
not of those slaughtered
savages
slaves
lesser peoples
eternally imprinted as nameless vessels
removed for construction

the human record
is not brimming with divinity
you must remember that

the gift of cleansing water
has escaped your eyes dear child
here
sit within shade
vines from trees above
will shield you from this energy

comfort is found in soft spaces
growing ivy engulfs your sadness
why do you weep
there is no audience to shame you

speak now
acknowledge this aftertaste
without wordy conjecture
purity of precision
tell of your troubles

your body quivers with hesitation
but please
you must divulge

the children
so young
fragile
exterminated for land

heritages erased with the brush of gentrification
colonization
for democratic nations

such turmoil
disturbing contradictions

wars sanctified as holy

if this is the legacy of mankind
what can our future possibly hold

violence as virtue
servitude as sacred
diversity as crimes of the highest accord
how forsaken a race we are
abolishing those we do not know
merely have not listened to

have we forgotten the touch of the breeze
gentleness found in whispers
tranquil illuminations in black skies above

where did we lose ourselves

what hope do we have
is there solace from such human treachery

keen inquiries indeed
primordial ponderings in fact
many have demanded solutions to these very problems
yet
none have ever been implemented
only fantasies
never given form

come
there is more to this tragic tale
walk you must
through this glen
into a sight you can not shy from
you must see to know
must witness to discern

in the near distance
you hear their chants
reverberating throughout roots around
tremble
does the ground

you are close

there
beyond last branch
a great gathering
angry ones

shouting with indistinctive unison
numerous
they stand around a fog-coated drop

center
suspended above the abyss
man-made form of torture
slicer of nobility
grand guillotine
hungry
ready to fall

you see
behold
lifesource of the cloth
human fallacies still breathing
festering around this pit
deep den of unashamed emptiness

there is no saving you from this crowd

through them you must journey

see their faces
know their names
hope for their souls to learn

prophetic fallacies

worlds above
or below
this is not certain

ones left
before venturing the Void
hatred seeps from their fingertips
even here
their reach is mighty
terrifyingly tangible

listen
for they speak of the plane you traveled from
watch
for they embody its actions
weep
for they know not what they do

as does an unexpected blow
words utter by this mass
mandate a daunting defenselessness
draining blood from your face
horror glazes your pupils

yes child

this is your world

a woman
sits near edge of the crowd
her skin
produces more melanin than those around her
without indication
men
women
and their children
consume the space around her peaceful figure

tearing at her arms
demanding she strip her flesh to match their own
she cries in agony
exposed veins ooze a sadness
tears do not even know
her shade is her epitaph
bones become still
those who want purification have taken another
deed done
left to sink into the sand
the woman lays mangled and motionless

behind her lifeless body
an intimate circle
possibly a family
revolves around two figures holding one another
mingled with the family shouting
each boy pleads to be heard
the woman spits upon her child
withdraws a dagger fashioned as a cross
piercing just below the shoulder
she extracts his heart
throwing the still-beating organ into the dirt
proclaims he does not deserve her love
he has blemished the meaning of matrimony
slumping to his knees
his lover reaches to his aid
the man nearest the woman
signals his god above
bellows with rage
cleanse this beast who stole my child
with this blade I pray
as the second body fell
the children gathered
giggle with sneering pride
damn the memory of their sibling to a place believed below

beside the slain men
a self-proclaimed church
approaches
praises god for their demise
they thrash placards
decorated with images
consecrated phrases
GOD HATES YOU
FORNICATION OF FAGGOTRY
PRAISE GOD FOR YOUR ENDING
believe their message is one of true salvation

from a podium
an unclear body
who has appeared throughout time in many forms
speaks with the voice of a man
the crowd gathered shouts
HAIL
HAIL to separation
construct a great divider
put them into compounds
incinerate their bodies
identify their heritage
burn their holy clothing
sacrifice them for our security

marching towards the guillotine
thousands covered in immaculate robes
hoods sewn into subtle points
resemble an army of angelic beings
contradicted by unseen faces
torches in hand
they chant of a morality they do not know

outlining rim of the pit
sleek row of connected boxcars
contain passengers idly in route to various destinations
among them
a woman
carries a thick backpack
she has chosen her fate
along with the hundreds aboard
releases soul from body
with pull of a cord
in papers they will deem her a terrorist
a leader will take responsibility
garnering prominence
basking in a fame from fear
interesting
how leaders never give their lives
only manipulate others to trade their own
in pursuit of power

men and women
firearms slung over their shoulders
laugh around trembling people
prostrate in the dirt
far from their platoon
innocent civilians pass the time
no one will miss them anyway

children play ring around the rosie
in the center
a solitary child protects their head
fetal position provides little safety
calling for someone
rocks bash their skin
the child will open a small bottle
swallows pills like salvation
no longer will their peers harm them
no longer will berating continue
they are free

a little boy
bound to branches in the dirt
a sick woman strikes a match
carefully nestles the open flame into his thick hair
the boy begins to burn
he has accepted this betrayal
calmly allowing the consumption of his frame
he does not fight what can not be undone
but who will speak for him
tell his story
those who could save
stand
watching
he was troubled they say
onto the body
a deceiver
drops a handmade necklace
into the scorching skeleton
twine falls through exposed ribs
landing beside what is left of his heart
with a final rasp
the child absolves those around him

reaching cessation of your procession
a horrid pulpit of jacobean walnut
fashioned on foundation of decomposing flesh
hardly living figures struggle under the weight
this structure demands
they bleed
weep for release
lessers in their rightful place
holding the hate they have been buried beneath

stage of skin
presides as gateway to the guillotine
assembled audience
thousands deep
exhilarated by a man upon the pedestal

he is the tender of torture
silencer of opposers
master of these masses

at his side
disciple of a foreign prophet kneels
solemn stature
she knows no shame
no misdeed has she performed
degradation is the price of her faith
with raising of arms
the man silences the crowd
for now he speaks

woe to thee
servant to satan
terror to the earth
opposer of truth
these vile creatures aim to redefine our creeds
ask for peaceful inclusion
silence all opposition we must
for it is written
to slice the abomination seekers
serfs can not learn to command their masters
us
superiors
appointed keepers of true knowledge
guardians of sanctified morality
this barbarism must crumble
with this woman
witness the cleansing crusade continue
prepare the sacred blade

eruption of accordance
sweeps through spectators
this is the sight which vindicates them
for collective erasure manifests perceived authority

a group of men and women
heave the shackled woman to her feet
turning her direction round
they lead her unto a bridge of twine and lumber
out toward the malicious machine
atop a swaying pillar
stone nor wood construct holder of the guillotine
rather
thousands of texts
spiraling downward through hanging mist
to unseen base below
holy books
theorized rationings
philosophical ponderings
heathens
heretics
traitors to the cause
cataloguing perversions of secular findings
library of opposition
twists up from the fog
capstone of grooves and steel
this dear child
is the guillotine of grandeur
fate of those who oppose any oppressor

do not close your eyes
do not turn away
stay here
you must see the decimation
to understand your purpose
this is your world
with disapproval comes reform
but with blind ignorance comes continuation
witness the events about to unfold

at long last
arrival on pillar platform
entourage hoists the woman onto a plank
suspended beneath knife
dangling

here
on soil of safety
crowds demand divine justice
this blasphemy of being
FINISH HER
CRUCIFY HER
END THIS TREACHERY

at a distance as great as your own
it is hard to detail the preparations

ferriers of this fate
bind the body to submission
extend her arms away from center
once steady
wrists are staked to wooden corners
nails piercing veins
sends waves of applause through the crowd below
sacred headwear
torn from her scalp
tossed from person to person
jests regarding monetary worth
are slung along with the fabric

positioning her chin upwards
she faces her jury
prying open her jaw
a man withdraws tongue from her mouth
aligned with sharpened steel
precision of mallot
leaves final nail to stretch bare muscle
under the shadow of its tormentor
a single tear plummets from her eyelid
muffled forgiveness to those below
escapes her esophagus

from above
metal is released

gravity takes hold
upon impact
an organ falls from oral nest
into abyss below

victory achieved
cheers resonate this chamber

now she can not speak her opposition
she must accept oppression without reproach
roughly untied
guards prop the woman to her feet
inaudible proposals
answer awaited by those gathered
she has chosen
again
the woman is turned
though she is lead to the other side of the platform
disapproval spewed from the crowd
as the woman embarks alone
across a duplicate bridge
spanning to an indistinguishable edge
other side no doubt

the crowd around
attends to their victims once more
until the next is to be silenced

there is but one way to the other side
dear child
you must approach the pulpit
your journey continues past the guillotine
it is your turn
remember
nor you
the woman
or countless before
have faced these fallacies alone

this road of the enlightened
requires travel in entirety

you must be strong
resolute

from behind
arms seize your shoulders

guillotine of grandeur

burly hands hold you firm
blocking blood from flowing past your elbows
spreading weakness through plasma canals
trembling to your knees
swaying
as does a redwood prepared to heave

do not stumble
grips will only intensify

led onward
you are presented to the preacher
the pulpit is petrifying before you
details you could not see from your prior place

elder eyes
gape from beneath lumber loads
long past terror
speak to you a soothing wisdom
reassuring you are not alone
you are not the first he has seen suffering

thrusting your spine in motion
you step onto the stage
from below
splitting bones harmonize
platform shifts
whimpers wheeze into the air
elder eyes gaze up
with a cracking peal
clavicles catapult from their cribs
accompanied with ichor and quiet sobbing

the man collapses
rejoices for temporary rest
disregarding throbs of skeletal agony

an onlooker
sees a lesser that has run its course
using unnecessary strength of foot
elder streamlines into the abyss
before dissolving under clouds
bliss illuminates a once-weary countenance
cortical wings
glide this man toward a veiled haven below

momentary distractions
interjected by a strike to your hamstrings
knee caps contact rigid floorboards
brought to a prayer you did not solicit
overhead
the preacher castigates

what is this
a conspirer with treason
lover to lessers
you are a disgrace to the purity we have been given
your very face is disgusting to behold
how dare you venture this journey
the road beyond is for heathens
perversions of humanhood
there is no need to continue on
this path has already been walked
you have been spared by one before you
that sacrifice suffices for those who listen

blasphemic vanity trickles from your pores
you clearly have chosen to meet the guillotine

this trespasser
decides not to trust in the message

with a gesture to your limp body
the preacher receives a grotesque applause from the horde

let us give this individual
the undeserving gift of salvation

expectorating onto your scalp
the preacher has given his blessing
now begins your trek to the guillotine

brought to your feet
a posse of men
women
even children
encircle you
forming an evenly distributed flanking
initiate your solemn tread
from behind
clamour rumbles in the air
anticipation spouts through the multitude

END THEM
SLICE THEIR PERVERSIVE TONGUE
BY THE GRACE OF DIVINE ORDINATION
CLEANSE THEIR SINS
PURGE OUR WORLD OF THEIR EVIL HANDS

upon the path
again you realize components unbeknownst before
under bruised feet
cartilage mingles with decaying organs
the railing
structure of interweaving bones
bound together by dismal entrails
no doubt
those previous
underfoot
each step
orchestrates hymn of degenerated humanity
sickening serenade of collective prejudice

such a painful reality
how humanity consumes humanity

vertex now in vision
jacobean walnut beams
sibling of the pulpit
elevates looming blade

scattered around base of the guillotine
trampled
discarded appendages litter the platform
tongues which did not fall into the abyss
abandoned by gravital grace
once-living linguistic devices
now fossilizing flesh
decolor to gloomy copper
forever marking the presence of their master

lethargically rotated
faced toward persecutors below
laid horizontally onto the center beam
accompanied by chants of the throng
your captors bind you

somewhere behind
iron trinkets chime
someone rummages for correct sizes
subsiding
they must have located suitable rivets

bellowing from beneath
the preacher
calls for fulfillment of your lesson

clenching your limbs
no strength left to wield
inaugural metal converges with your heel
warm liquid seeps into your skin
yet you feel no pain

how is this so
is your body numb to the point of passiveness

answer spirals your mind into a nauseous state
they do not clean the piercers

as fresh blood from another soul
cascades across your shin
nail is pressed deeper
with a deafening pound
metal enters unsuspecting tissue
writhing in anguish
your mind barely registers the first puncture
before a second nail burrows into raw flesh

as though submerged in ocean depths
sound becomes distant
muffled
chin compressed into wood
opening your mouth to wail
teeth scrape strings of bark into your mouth

your arms are stretched to maximum length
palms twisted outward
simultaneous injections
herald final horrid penetration

through culminating tears
a delicate figure approaches you
mallet in hand

a small girl
cherub no longer merciful
innocence robbed from her
reared among hatred

for the process of persecution
is an artform which must be passed down

she glares into your blurring eyes
with a grin she cradles your jaw
lifting your head to gods above
pray for her soul to one day learn

no longer obscured by timber
you see the mass clapping in unison
they do not know you
yet they desire your demise

the young girl
pries into your mouth
her fingers taste of sand and salt
extracting your tongue from hidden burrow
attempts of resistance
bring a sharp slap from her smooth palm
her paradoxical conduct
pains you more than the intruders in your veins

she unfolds your tongue
positions muscle
levitating nail
like last raindrop falling from desert skies
she angles the mallot

witnessing erasure of innocence
you see her eyes
devoured by haunting glee
as nail plummets through its target
just as the woman before you
a single tear is released
as you internally plead

forgive her
let her see the pain she is inflicting
learn this is no salvation

like a gorgeous tapestry is slit
by those who do not know its worth
sheet of steel
followed by exposed muscle
are liberated from their place of beginnings

thousands erupt in approval
stench of rusting metal fills your nostrils
as liquid brims over your lips
dripping off the beam
soaking tongues below
mixture of rose and titian
appearing almost alive again

among puddles of molding murk
the foot of a young child

discards your fallen flesh

deep into the darkness below

voices rise from the mist

chilling stillness washes through the air
members of the mass await your answer
the very question asked of all who are silenced

once again
the girl approaches
gaping into your drying irises
she coos

you may now choose
to join us in our crusade to salvation
become a light-bearer for true messages

or

you may foolishly embark onward
into caverns of damnation
once again decide to relinquish eternal prosperity
disregard our courtesy of saving your soul
for pathways of heathens

the choice
is for you alone

take a moment if you desire
dear one

however
your exodus is far from conclusion
there is still much to witness
but
as the child said
choosing is solely upon you

apparent in your demeanor
your decision
is met with uproars of degradation from below
as with the woman before you
captors release your body
lead you to beginning of the second bridge

aggressively shoved
you have displeased their charity
they unshackle you from their hospitality

initially stumbling forward
you begin sprinting
viaduct of solidified marrow and twine
swaying beneath your rhythm

afar
safety in nearing road
flee this place
the pit below
crowds behind
such an objective is understandable

wait
there in the air
voices are whispering
not from behind
but every which way
slicing deep into your cranium

failure
barbaric disgrace *unworthy*

vocalizing breezes
choruses sing of your misdeeds
judgements upon your character
falsehoods regarding your life
listen to their deception
but do not entice them to take form
for their grasp is not one which gifts freedom

your life has been a waste
such a shame that you still breathe

earth would find contentment
if you hurled yourself from this suspension

the evil in this world is not what you just witnessed
it lives within your heart
the hatred you feel
oh such jealously
self-pity
disgusting squander of flesh and bone
never
shall you amount to hollow aspirations you hold

an excuse of pulse waves
violater of purity
destroyer of propriety

relieve the world of your presence
slaughter yourself
before you wreak multitudes of havoc
greater than you already have

you have tainted this universe
your perversive personhood
leaves a putrid stench in your wake
cleanse us of you
leave now
let this world breathe fully once more

dear child
confront the voices
silence their heinous accusations
surely you must know they render falsely
command this chamber with your own voice

but I lack means to form words
my very tongue has been purloined
ripped from crevice of my mouth
blood floods
even now
I could not possibly utter a mere coherent sound

there is where you are wrong love

yes
guardians of the guillotine defiled your tongue
however

absolute silencing of one
cannot be obtained through human constructs

a tongue is a tongue
a voice is a grander
separate entity

they can only take from you
what you believe you have given them

now speak
command this cavern
crowds behind you
voices around
everyone must hear your declaration
ordain yourself with the strength they could not take
a power rooted in noiseless resistance

rise

rise with these aggressors
lift yourself above invalid accusations

cowering
you suggest these words have not swayed you

with cautious motion
you spread your lips
as a lion prepares to roar into dusty savannas
with trembling exultation

simple word spills from your throat

silence

as light radiates from every pore
locution emits into the air
with graceful grandness
your body levitates
up from platform of oscillating planks
into heavens above

arms outstretched as the wings of a cardinal
such illumination appears fire has consumed your figure
again you emanate vibrations

hear me now

those beyond

those above

those below

silence

for
now

I am speaking

dust unto dust, flames become ashes

how fickle

conversion is

capacity of commands
by vibration of your lips

burning has begun

cleansing of purity

deluging flame

shutters through those below
twisting into radiant orbs

reach to your toes

as even you are enveloped
shimmering
theses of your own accord

scholars say your parturition is one of ancient ash

amalgamation of nova lineage

cosmic continuation

below
malicious masses
circularly spiral upwards

particles

peacefully peeling into novel form
ashes must unrestrictedly dance

once a brilliant ember
turned travelers of wind

humanity in unblemished form

never forget this moment
dear one

burning along with those below
reborn in uncontained being
you are one with the breeze

this is your time

do not condemn the fallacious ones

rather

impart the wisdom
running through your veins

even now

speak your musts

temporal luminous

inchoation of your ministry

light-bearer to the truth

embodiment of palpable goodness

speak

say

what

you must

for

you

must

they

must

hear

you

Invocations

upon the sight of divinity

one must gaze within

and without

burning balance

behold
by whisk of wind
abrupt burnings
fade

dwindle into plateau likeness
sheet of shimmering cinder
eonic equilibrium

dense fog
one of tangible tranquility
awakens through the ground
levitating as from a deep slumber
gracefully polluting air
silky stillness

quiet softness
circulating ashes
could be mistaken as snowfall
cast a melancholic warmth
peculiar comfort

where such horrendous sights
human injustice once stood
built upon bones
fueled by fear
now great field
fertile hollowness
awaits new purpose

an arboretum of healthy saplings
life-givers
shall be sown
perhaps

only time
holds answer to this vacancy

come
you must continue

there
erosion in chamber wall
provides a passage onward
sliver of space
forces lateral movement
tight enclosure
covered by cavern darkness
stones scrape your checks
temples
hips
tearing into flesh

let hands guide you
feel yourself forward
unaware of ceiling height
keep head low

sudden dip
sends cranium into contact
you shudder with a stupor
bashed by the stumble
vertigo pushes you on

incision ahead
exposes an iridescent cerulean
with end near
foul stenches creep into the air

fighting into the light
you emerge from small spaces
only to heave

at such a sight

unholy figurehead

mammoth beast before you
suggests the guillotine was merely consented ecstasy

twirling tongues of acid conflagration
lick twelve lips
potent fangs crown cartilage creases
jutting with lack of symmetry
folding back into grim gullet gloom

burgundy fumes revolve around nostrils
dripping blood of another

juxtaposing the ferocious fiend
silver slits
contain ethereal irises
cut from sacred stone
swirling sapphires
fruit of Andaman comber

gorgeous terror
sirenic serenade
piercing your soul

holding twelve hideous heads
spiked shoulders slump
nephrite curvatures
rest atop a disillusioning form

descending from forearms
deficiency of flesh
instead
body of mirage

flashes of another likeness
another story

your story

this creature
known to you many times before
entity of transgressions
haunting choices
peoples who wounded you
catalogue of catastrophe

you must confront this demon
disconnect ropes it has anchored
within your soul

only by slaying this brute
can you be freed
unshackled from these weights
past follies
previous abuses
falls you did not anticipate
breakings you believed binding

before the atrocious figure
senses your presence
erase its essence
dispel any power it holds
conquer this demon within you
existing only to torment

alas
perturbation must be recognizable
for with fearsome force
the demon lashes out
cuffing you into unbalanced motion

with a dreadful cry
you fall to the ground

timidly crawling
cowering to safety
behind a boulder
shielded from sight

panting
you sputter words

I can not prevail here
recollections of my past tribulations
this demon is one of my own making

I created its lifeline
by my hand only
this creature remains
now my hands are too weak
to rewrite what has been written
take this trial from before me
let it pass
let it no longer be

dear child
this beast will no longer be
if you deem it so
solely by your prevail
can peace finally be known

this trial alone
is for you to engage
with blinding confidence
unparalleled strength
can you undo
what you have let fester

come
stand before the demon
gaze into cyan eyes
those which have witnessed all that you have

command its departure from your veins
no longer allowed to plague unwilling host

static
you remain hunched in refuge
curled as child in womb
praying closed eyes will vanquish this place
take you back to warmth of familiarity
safety to greet you like an old friend

dear one
you must know by now
safety is such a subjective serenity
facade of reality
to truly know safety
you must face the greatest forms of peril

here
before you now
paramount of danger
for it is a figurehead built by your own accord

how greater an act of love
then to forgive yourself

defeat final obstacle
erase burdens of this heavy load
only then can you move onward
continue this journey
for that is the paramount of safety
equilibrium of self-doubt and worth
obtained

you must stand before this siren
end what you began
regain command of your soul once more

quite petrified
you do not stir
overcome by dubiety
you can not envision a possible feat

take a moment
concentrate back to initial errors
performed when you were young
impregnation of this agonizing weight
where did this demon take first form
cardinal regret
foundation of further growth

go back there
smell the air as it was
listen to the sounds around you
feel remorse flow through you one last time

now
take that contrition
let elimination of this darkness
be penance

channeling an aged yearning
to finally alleviate yourself from this nostalgic presence

you rise
step out from behind boulder
stare into icy pupils

with thunderous magnitude
you shout

be gone
I demand you depart from this place
I no longer give you command over my soul
to beset my thoughts
I reclaim my home

you are not welcome here
leave
trouble me never more

as final sonorous timpani beats
shutter to conclude orchestral scores
once towering fiend
buckles
crumbling to cinders

debris swirling into transparent clouds
protruding from rubble
elegant twins glisten

fetch the orbs
detached from impious sockets
no longer capable of harm

keep them as tokens
remembrance of victorious battle
dislodging that which possessed you
held you captive
prevented restoration from occurring

unseeable before
barricaded by demonic body
pathway into fecund taiga

there
among growth of green
resides a place
where your journey
reaches climax
divine metamorphosis
forthcoming

a dove. above

overhead

giver of compromise
divine atonement
spiritual validation

wingspan immaculately unfurled
without stain of insincerity
insult to pure hue

heralds a saturating peace

the Void

has heard your cries
seen your toils
wept for your turmoil

validates your struggle
importance of these learnings

this messenger
indicates you are ready
prepared to know a deific death
sacred sacrifice
fulfillment of your purpose

you have witnessed
you have cleansed

now you must learn
experience

only then
can one obtain
plethora of universal knowledge

true understanding
unsullied compassion
absolute humanness

bringing with its presence
soothing spirit
palpable pulse

from wingtips
calming dusk spreads into the air

though this is not night
for time is forsaken here

stillness and serenity
swallow the Void

come
you may rest

lay arbor

into the thicket
embrace of sprawling branches above
carpet of shade
makes for a place to settle

lay your head on soothing sod
listen to heartbeats
thump melodiously through roots below

you have prevailed
against mighty adversities
dozing is for you to relish
glide into gratifying slumber

close your eyelids love
grant yourself a moment
recollect strength of mind
aptitude of spirit
for soon
imminent circumstances require
utmost vigor

acquiring appropriate degrees of verve
demands surrender into dream realms
partake in this necessary exercise

worry not
submission into subconsciousness
will not go unprotected
no harm shall wage upon you
while you drift

however
harm waged within you
can not be prevented
there are no methods to shield
one from their own mind

with sudden jolt
eyes flutter open
spine springs into upward motion
adjusting view
you begin to calculate your surroundings

still beneath spiraling oaks
recognizable ground
recollecting how you came to be
in this place

time offers no aid
as light has not progressed
absence of luminescent measurement
you might deduce time has passed
though unsure of quantity

if you must know
the spectrum clocks command
has not run a long course in your absence
mere minutes in fact

you must be famished
parched
admittingly
you have undergone considerable ordeals

further into the forest
promisingly contains
some form of nutrition

after wandering
aimlessly through luscious boscage
pleasant discovery presents itself

collection of shrubs and bushes
speckled by hanging bulbs
growth of wild berries will suffice
in forage for edible items

gather sizeable rations
stow succulent fruits in cupped palms
cradle shirt as pouch
clasped by stretching cloth to pinched teeth
providing maximum volume
for future likelihood of finding more
is quite slim

few steps further
reveal an uncovered clearing
subjected to open air
ground bathed by nonexistent ceilings

profound significance
permeates scattered pebbles
discarded sticks strewn about

the space is almost questionable
incongruent configuration
mysteriously concealed
within such palatial brush

although dubious at primary glances
this enclosure is adequate as momentary lounge
feasting on delicious gains
though lacking diversified options
poses a redundant palate

venturing into the gaping area
you analyze surrounding wall of trees
perfectly planted in a wide circle
symmetrical length to any given outlying point
curiously mesmerizing
evidently intentional
but with what rationale

unclear purpose
leaving usage relative to one currently present
a single place
with infinite intentions

chaos
restrained in firm absolute
concurrently
an absolute
distressed with bearing perpetual chaos

as with painted canvas
human mind
fertile sphere of inhabitants

existent in concrete purity of form
though reliant upon
disorder to project order
identity built on cultivating idiosyncratic aspects
compounded to form singular entity

never altering origin
but unrestricted to dictate destinations

here there be unblemished balance
world without skewed scale
equipoise of living and dying

for dying

is only the whittling of yesterdays

and living

is carving new lumber on the morn

sacred land
brimming natural holiness
where worshippers find fulfillment
amidst absence of icons
distracting relics

synagogue of internal stimulus
mosque of introspection
cathedral of bark and turf
temple for aboriginal meditation
praise in purest form

solely a soul
and silence

nearby
a rustle stirs
snapping twigs
echoing through treetops
suggest someone has materialized

desiring to join you in this hollow clearing

simple shrine

from beyond the grove
approaches a meager trio
shadows of your previous witnessings

child
man
woman

plodding toward this clearing
among the trees

contrary to before
they descend upon you
undeniable joy-marked faces

weariness
strife
washed away
fulfillment found in following this trek
experiencing a Void apart from your own
yet one of same substance

first
the woman
reaches you

extending her arms
engulfs you with shaking grasp
beginning as a small whimper
she starts to sob tears of gratitude
among droplets dripping down cheeks
words are released from her throat
words which have waited millennia for life

by your valor
ways you have paved
what I have endured with you

I have seen the strength in suffering
learned to let go of questioning
that which has been answered
accept things I can not alter
erase burdens that shackled me firm
cease searching
for what is right before me
allow myself to heal from the past
instead of spending eternity locked within prior follies

for that
I am unfathomably grateful

after final tightening grip
she releases you
bending forward
places a kiss on your brow
before relinquishing the forefront

next
the man
stands
studying your face
tears trickling down his own
such raw content
without speech
he says a great deal
until he too
embraces you
followed by voicing sentiments

how
I do not know

yet
your journey and subsequently mine
have given me a gift
I long ago deemed unobtainable

one will never find greatest forms of praise
in books
dogmas
rituals
or even the lack of these things

whether one is searching for a deity
morality
secular healing
no matter the cause
epitomes of veneration
are found in valuing the universe around me
universe within me
and accepting these notions as enough

loosening his hold
briefly gazes into your eyes once more
nodding with sincerity
he joins the woman

finally
the child
who remained still
arms wrapped behind them
while comrades spoke

peers up
lingering in place
quietly staring

this time
unfolding your own arms
attempts to beckon the child to find shelter
within your opened frame
go unaccepted

still
the child does not move

instead
stretching from behind
they bring forth
that which was hidden

a casket
very one being buried
when you found them

timidly displaying the object in their hands
the child looks down upon the wooden case

with ease of hand
the casket falls from its nest
gently settling onto thick grass

as wood plummets
the child scurries into your arms

lifting them up
you spin into circular dance
tears breaking across your face
as they do upon their own

hold them
celebrate in their finding of certainty
ending of their searching
their pain

hold them close
for you were once them
and as time progresses on
they will become you

slowly succumbing to exhaustion
you place them upon the ground

returning to the sides of fellow wanderers
the child bends forward
retrieving that which they discarded

along with the child
the man extracts a book from trouser pocket
missing pages
crumpled and maltreated spine
hold a binding
once fit for a sanctuary

the woman reaches into her thick coat
withdrawing a mangled collection of ropes
useless net
for a large hole
diminishes purpose
cursed to never capture
objects below surfaces

from clenched fist
you expose two stones
eyes for a once terrifying varmint
epitaph of reclaimed personhood

with trio of roamers
bring your items
trinkets which brought unceasing torment
incapable of closure
to final a resting place

laid forth
upon the ground
center of this clearing

simple shrine
one to commemorate
toil transformed triumphs
of souls over their past

beatification of souls

beyond intimate circle
from dense treeline
a great mass emerges from behind bark pillars

pieces of prolonged failures
hoisted by proud shoulders
piles of rotting worries
torments of human worthiness
epidemics of shortcomings

demons
masquerading as objects
polluting moments
uniquely known to each individual
haunting falls from past decisions

as more process into the clearing
laying their burdens
at the base of a towering heap
a gleaming begins to crackle from the accumulation
multiplying in size
intensity of light

until
a most beautiful metamorphosis betides
once vile remnants
bloom a resplendent making

consecrated festival

glorious feast

hallowed ground

locus where your ancestors speak their wisdom

banquets sprawled upon granite tables
violet-lined lanterns hover above
violaceous illumination warms the air

bread of wheat
sown upon the Nile

bulging bowls of Yangmei berries
nestled near dishes of Khoresh
turmeric wafting in pleasant breezes

chalices dripping
drink from Eurasian barrels
glisten by the glow of dusk

meats from Northern plains
fruits from Southern mountains
Plantains
Guavas
Mangos
lusciously crown
polished plates

upon a raised platform of golden dandelions
a gathering of musicians harmonize
rhythms of distinct cultures
linger as one
producing an orchestra of purity in plurality

upon the ground
more bouquets of dandelions
line a wide dancefloor

among them
pirouetting figures
originating of all lands
move to the composition of sacred melodies

unashamed
unrestricted
permission unneeded
to express their souls

bodies contort
spin
spiral
leap
land
duplicate

such grace
such beauty
unworried humanness
shackles removed
burdens forgotten

rebuilt
into eternal source of jubilation
to celebrate
one another
without malice
or judgement

merely to be
and let be

sacred splendor manifests
when the human lineage
holds the weight together

proceed
dear one
join them
for they are your family
and you of them

rejoice
amongst your cosmic kin

stumbling
overcome with admiration
you step into the gathering

into vision
come familiar sights

faces
from distant dreams

no
a daunting cloth
unfurling somewhere in time

they dance here
now

children from native nations
play with the children of their tormentors
sculpting palaces from soil
catching fireflies
giggling into uncontrolled fits
bruised no more
eyes bright as the stars above a faraway world
genocide did not prevail
sharing their wisdom
not listened to before

mangled bodies
cast into pits
mass graves
chambers continued to supply
move unhindered
inscribed numbers

erased from forearms
beam at the children they left behind
at the children who left with them
a people who have found their home

young children
with melanin-kissed bodies
run through tall grass
eating sweets
allowed to be young
not targeted
not profiled
unafraid to exist in their skin
their mothers eyes
peer loving unto them
fathers arms
outstretch toward them

an old man
whose body was snapped
kicked into an abyss
sits with the very one
who discarded him effortlessly
together they share life stories
where they came from
where they were going
who they wanted to be
who they had become
eventually embracing
this sight
sends chills of affirmation
down your aching spine

a tearful mother
sits with her child
lover by his side
holds the hand of her child

the very one slain
by blade of her words
in her other hand
rests the palm of his lover
unbroken circle
healed with vulnerable surrender

when love is enough

from within the dancing figures
a singular soul emerges

a woman
tongue stripped by the masses
abandoned to putrefy
steps into view

vibrant silk gown
flows from her shoulders
when she walks
a monarch train gracefully lingers
demanding the soft fabric to ripple

extending her hands outward
she greets you with a kiss upon each cheek
as though you are old companions
but you truly are

for all who know the Void
see the potency
of the struggle within another

clasping your hands
she leads you onto the dancefloor
amidst sanctified euphoria

swaying about
alongside the gathering
you and the woman twirl
eventually
space is cleared
the crowd exhilarates you
clapping
pace quickening
gliding in balanced unison
faster
faster

looking up
you see her beaming
her legs begin to sidestep
landing heel to beat
toe to pause

as the song wanes
she guides your spin to a slow swing
before departing
brings you inward
for an amiable embrace

stepping back
from center
you once more peer upon the festivities

to the side there is a table
decadently displayed cups
bowls of juice and drink

you approach
pouring yourself a generous gulp
taste buds rejoice
the swig is as though someone drained sunlight
squeezed celestial brilliance into fluid form

nearby
a collection of carved stumps
provide a place to sit
nestling in
you relax and discern
examining the spectacle unfolding

palpable tranquility
unquestioned dignity
equal worthiness

blessed congregation
mingling
despite past mistakes
decisions
horrendous deeds

forgiven
absolved

what kind of bliss could this be
surely this is not truly possible
not in the realities that exist
beyond this clearing

witnessing this beauty
realizing this space as tangible
truly possible
sends a passionate ache
throughout your very veins within

taking a second helping
of galactic libations
emotions fester
lowering the cup from your lips
you allow words
to take form

where was this goodness
moments ago

where was the scaredness
millennia prior

before the seeds of separation
zygote of emptiness
began to grow
ultimately maturing into such disdain
forgetting the moment when all was balanced
all was of the same
is of the same

when was the cloth cut
divided into fragments
only fractions
of the magnificence it could be

why does humanity
choose
to defy this splendor
reverence of virtue

how shameful
that this atmosphere
this very space
feels far more inhuman
than of human likeness

the humanity I know
collective presence beyond
act in no way comparable
this tenderness I now bear
does not exist
how can it
there is no place for it to dwell within

oh
dear one
for this is the greatest sorrow
humanity holds

the goodness
love
potential for sacred solidarity
was always present
merely never given full due

just imagine
for a moment
if the world you left beyond
reflected a beauty
such as this
when goodness
is given full measure to build

yet take heart
for now
solely a glimpse
of what the world was meant to be
can be witnessed in the events about to transpire
hold these proceedings close

do not dismiss them
shepherd others to this hallowed space
so they too
can know what divinity manifest
utmost sacred sacrifice

enlightens
awakens
and burns

within you

wicks and wax

from within the great mass
emerges a small figure
the child
you have come to remember
while walking this pathway
nears your place
resting apart from others

without noise
no spoken greeting
the child sits at your feet

plucking a minuscule weed
growing among luscious grass
slowly they detach yellow petals
from warmth of receptacle base
fluttering to the floor

remaining silent
until
for the very first time
they speak to you

what is bothering you
why are you sad

smiling
for even you can not fathom an answer
to such an elementary inquiry

I am not sure how I am feeling
but I do not think I am sad
just frustrated

what about you
how are you feeling

pausing
before they respond
the child extracts a final petal
left with nothing
but a skeleton
once blooming plant

I am not sure either
I never expected to feel such kindness
as I do here
all these people are so good to me
I almost do not trust them
why would they be like this
they do not even know my name

again
you find yourself unable to reply
for you are pondering
these very same questions

before an answer is entertained
footsteps herald a newcomer
the woman
with whom you danced prior
proceeds to invite your pairing
back among the crowd

obliging
you and the child stand
clasping hands
your trio returns to the festival

upon arrival at populated edge
a pounding drumbeat
hushes all noise
pulsates a silent magnitude

one of preparation

where tables
food and drink
festivities stood
dissolve
as mysteriously as they appeared

remnants levitate
collecting in one centered spherule
glowing soothing silver
swirling like creamy milk

all gathered
from each hand
a candle
brought forth
hungry for flicker

through the silence
the child
rustles leaves upon the ground
as they step forward

whisper a name you call your own

Child

exact moment
when syllables lept from their mouth
orb bends
string of light
connecting with waiting wick
in their palms
bursting candle into life

the woman nearest the child
steps forward for lighting
with heated contact
comes audible word

Nurrin

beside her
she passes flame to a new figure
upon receiving her gift
he speaks

Muhammad

following prior patterns
he extends the singular bulb of light
to the tip of neighboring candle
as the flame grows in radiance
so too
does the revelation of names

Nathaniel

Anastasia

Valencia

Iman

Diyan

Immanuel

Olivia

Irena

Abraham

Aliza

Chakir

Jasura

Amani

Solomon

Anthony

Stellan

Hannah

Tamir

Beatrix

Mehr

Aksha

Pelia

Zelig

Benedict

Thaddeus

Sachi

Mireya

Barbara

Sophia

Naomh

Chenaanah

Deirdre

Azizi

Ishmael

James

Dhruva

Ariel

Bodhi

Grace

Magdalena

Hope

Caiyun

Jur

Clarence

Ruya

Sakina

Wafi

Ziya

John

Ann

Pax

Jason

David

Tambika

Kai

Rose

Ling

Ayasha

Ninovan

Tatianna

Kachina

Yazmin

Ezra

Umar

Sylvia

Fatima

Quinn

Xavier

though no instrument plays
no melody of sound
emits from the surrounding air
names read
split the atmosphere
with haunting reverence

Mikal

names
such formidable applications
when physicality
spirit
ancestry
and identity
ordain a single word

Prisha

language can not even contain
definitions for these holy utterings
what is for one
can not carry what is for another

Waseme

names
vowels
consonants
inflections
tongue and saliva
annunciate
far more powerful entities
than the noise they produce

Catori

each instance
when spoken
written
envisioned
paradox of institution
constituted pinpoint
ordered blueprint

Upala

a name

is a pulse
memory
an earthquake
flood

Emmett

a sunset on the last morning
sunrise on the first

Adam

is a heartache
a road
a death
a life
a Void

Gabriel

a record of human progression
enshrined
between grapheme measurement
called forth
with each utterance

Miriam

you must always know
memorize
recite
validate
monikers of the human family

Diego

each is a prayer
a birthright
a eulogy

an essence

to deny one their name
negates their capacity
disregards triumphs
erases struggles
blasphemous crime

Shanti

to indulge another
invoking anything less
then their core truth
sacrilege
cruel
ignorant
for if you do not know the name
you can never see
witness
experience
the soul embedded within

Joseph

as every name
spoken by its vessel
echoes
illumination swells
mammoth ring of flame
daunting in size
magnificent nuances
reflected in illumined countenances
heights
skin hues

Habiba

accentuate contrasts
subtle and distinct

Charlie

variations not revealed by light
dialect-licked tongues
coarse strikes
silk glides
curling rings

Winifred

pay homage
to those centuries ago
diasporas
migrations
map movements
settlements
displacements
faulty assimilation
when cultures survive

Sabihah

it is imperative
to comprehend
in a world
which shall strip some of their worth
devouring valuation
besieged bodies
all one has left
is the power of their name

Maya

how holy such an entity becomes
intimate
venerable
unparalleled

Abel

for even deities
have names

Elizabeth

passing orb continues
radiance spilling
isomorphic structure
balancing circuit
awaiting sealing by
last spoken word

with unlit wick
you remain still
complete awe
undeniable admiration
for unfurling meaning

amongst you

baptismal blaze

here is heaven

laid before you
mightily humble
unshaken

holy in hope
divine by design
bound with beauty

for always remember
dear one
darkness shall be consumed
even by solitary flame

as with flame
there is goodness in the universe
even if nourished by only one pulse

take comfort
in knowing this truth

William

mother orb
hanging center
continues gifting irradiated threads
to each wick bearer

Kelila

as web of a spider
nest of the dove
fragmented lines amalgamate circular haven

Peter

gazing upon orb eye
you are brought
to nonexistent memories
communal longing

Heather

flashing depictions
events illusory
for these images
did not come to pass
history begging
to be rewritten
forgotten
scrubbed clean
but
keep the cracked remembrance
or repetition shall be your tomb

Agnes

portrayals
siblings to a cloth
peered upon prior
swirl in metamorphic manner

a crusade
Urban anointed
disbanded
instead
a brilliant institution
erected on a hill
where learning ensued
eager empathy incited understanding
holy trinity of faiths
familial lineage
descendants of a nomadic people

human dignity
enacted from the beginning

peoples of color
aboard ships
unshackled
spacious interiors
populate a new world
alongside paler faces

native lodgings do not burn
trails are not walked
a world built together
sacred lands are not industrialized
leaders reflect greater populous

oligarchies never take root
wealth distributed mercifully

genocides know no life
warfare is myth
humanity knew from the start
goodness is paramount
the Void is actualized

cultures remain
ungentrified
revered as sanctified

churches constructed
next to mosques
beside temples
across from laboratories
academic institutes
debates never turning violent
only passionate

children laugh
abuse unknown
given room for unhindered growth

mass graves
undug
gaseous chambers never built

death is not feared
purposes unquestioned

femininity is sacred
not submissive
no master to heed

history books
speak of environmental nourishment
care for the ground given
foolish people
busy with establishing tall buildings
shiny roads
without considering
weight they exude
on the frail spine of spherical core

a dove

soars above a village in Africa
healthy children skip to drumbeats
bustling cities echoing ancestral hymns
glides among concrete labyrinths
upon the ground
people are walking
laughing
speaking with one another

hovers over a rainforest in America

campos emit smoke rings
falling dusk
whispers of elders
telling stories
oral traditions
triumphs of their people
vitality despite hardship

flutters amongst mighty temples
hanging atop monstrous mountains
where silence breathes a cosmic inhale
meditations
chants
exhales

plummets into swaying paddy fields
north into Eurasian icicles
gumdrop-crowned cathedrals
isolated huts
flame-licked windows
connect to cobblestone passageways

twirling in between highrises
wafting Golonka
Arabian Coffee grounds
fresh Halawa

sputtering railways below
slither into city centers
towering clock strikes
reverberating unto river surfaces beneath

turning
your bird passes a dusty savanna
pyramids pierce heavens
a sea swirls
amid lush emerald waves upon land

hitting an invisible barrier
winged beauty
enters a familiar space
from above
you witness the descent

the fledgeling
has entered this Void
streamlining through the air
they plunge in the clearing

without slowing
cracking
sphere of light
ruptures
electrifying intensity of already burning flames

reciting names elevate
circle nearing cessation

returning your focus
to those around you
remember
images provided by global wingspan
can be unwritten future
do not dwell in the unchangeable
thrive in the tangible
healable pathway forward

by step of your toes
rhythm of your breath
movement of hands
forever strive
painstakingly
unapologetically
to summit the terrifying incline
of human possibility

once surfaced
gaze out
upon land promised
those who seek goodness
room for all humanity

this is your baptism
divine cleansing
when you see
what could be

if all is actualized with serenity
sincerity
prosperity
love
goodness

in the far distance
final name is made audible
translation of this unbroken bloodline

Amaziah

but alas
a single name remains unspoken
you dear child
without your title
circle can not combine
ceremony incomplete
so speak
speak dearest one
with a smooth tongue flick
syllables you know most well
your

Name

pyre of pressed twigs

votives in hand
the gathering spreads out
without breaking webbing above
divinity evident
venturing into woods around
all returning with carvings in unoccupied palms

following suit
you turn
and process into tree lining

upon trunk surfaces
gorgeous symbols
emblazoned
ancient markings
all depictions of a greater narrative

a wheel
with eight protruding spokes
whirls in mesmerizing fashion
speaks of a divine space
where all will peer into themselves
all should seek
all could find

Nirvana

immediately left
upon a different tree
unfathomably desecrated
defiled to the utmost of shame
spirals with four legs
sings a solemn tale of well-being
when humanity misuses the gifts it is given
echoing through time

still more boles hold
symbols known to many
as representations
of Voids past

a cross
where a man hung
bound by hatred
willing to suffer
for all to learn
promises of redemption
cognitive revival
masters of life and death
sacredness in self-sacrifice

Resurrection

a star
twin triangles converge
tell a tale of sand and water
of a burning bush
a promise made
journey begun
Adonai
I Am
We Are
One

Chosen

a green mist
shimmers into a crescent moon
from bare space
between tail tips
a star materializes
before dissolving into hues of jade
once more

patterns shifting symbol
changing meaning
as time progresses
murmur of a mountain cave
when a man
was given a message
one rhythmically transcribed to his people

Inner Struggle

steps further
you discover an intricate grouping of spheres
spurting from rims
arrows
crosses
lines
each circle
looping through one another
creating an ever-moving spectrum of colors
rainbow of sorts
conglomerate of personhoods

Identity

to the right
feather with fashioned tip
drips ink
lingering thoughts
unwritten words
universes awaiting awakening
from a literary master
who can conjure
from the deepest crevices of their mind
spawning life
lustrous canons of written grandeur

Magnum Opus

upon neighboring tree
simple instrument
carved wood
infused bristles
dipped in natural dyes
crescendos of color
composition of catastrophe
brought forth into resounding imagery

Self-Portrait

a whirling assortment of orbital progress
centered nucleus
reverence of empirical consistency
electron kissed magnitude
science as physical pattern
order of ways
truth can be found in sight
majesty in human capacity
knowledge
pathway of inquirers

Heuristic

a fist
cracked skin
worn with age
unshackled wrist
firmly heralding a freed vision
rooted in those before
dreams
change
let it ring
spirits of movements bygone
marching present

Liberation

a bottomless tremor
bellowing apart from time
primordial melody
chord of first chorus
sweeping through cosmic continuation
divinity
reverberating within itself
apart from itself
sacred circulation

Om

resting on a final tree
humble curvatures
suspended center
thickened circle
enclosed around
large similar circumference
all encompassed
by a quadrilateral
musings to aboriginal lands
comprehensions of holiness personified

the Void depicted
in earliest tapestries
sewn of the buffalo
molded of clay
guided by starlight
ancestors above

for those who search
shall find what they seek
but those who wander
will stumble upon sacredness
unbeknownst prior

Great Spirit

as a wanderer
you too have entered this space
among the trees
unanticipated
unsure

however
now
you must choose the symbol
exterior mirroring of your very soul

perhaps
your essence is revealed
within previous Voids
a marking witnessed before
in the trunks surrounding you

or
perhaps you will happen on
a more potent sign
representing the Void you find yourself upon

continue searching
among the bark
until you have found
most satisfying portrayal

this question is given an answer
as you come to gaze
onto the very embodiment of your truth

like the images
reflecting on the growths around
levitating ahead
inscribed absolutes

You

retrieve yourself
dear one
approach the tree
peel away your epigraph
with unimpeded palm
hold yourself

rejoin the others

entering the clearing once again
you notice most have returned
overhead
pulsating web
has not dwindled
only gathered strength

eventual stragglers
fill empty spaces
signaling fulfillment of all returning

preparations begin
as a figure breaks from their position
candle in hand
symbol in other
moves toward nucleus

aloft
trail of light
extending from their wick
travels as they do
merging into the middle
laying their wooden object down
they remain
fixating upon its surface

gradually
others begin joining them

with each person
journeying inward
bands of radiance upward
multiply
intertwining into a wide warmth

go to them
dearest one
lay your personhood upon the earth
gift that which is you
to the swelling group there

behold

your sacred sacrifice
crucifixion
enlightenment
rebirth
deific death

destiny of all

heeding advice given
you step closer to the crowd center
quicken pace
you begin to sprint
feet thumping
body clumsily forced forward

stumbling
you fly onto the ground
mud-caked
bruises already forming
frame aches
from hardened contact

but no matter
you have reached your destination

unable to stand
palpable power
meaning of this people
demands your body
relinquish command

surrender
for healing can not ensue
unless you are not in control

remaining prostrate
you crawl final meters
keeping your head positioned down

initially slow dripping
succumbs to spilling tears
you begin to sob
as you arrive upon the pyre

feeling unworthy
unfit to look upon this holiness
absolute embodiment of all gathered
raw
battered
hopelessly hopeful humanity
you still do not lift your head

merely present your essence
your symbol
you
to be laid alongside the others
gifts before a divine nativity

birth of goodness

sensing a presence
drawing near to you
shadows on the ground confirm suspicions
though you stay still

until
a fragile fingertip
caresses your cheek
gently raising your face to meet their own

the child
reminds you of a young girl
who held you in a familiar position
eons ago
on a horrendous pillar
beneath sheet of steel

how different this moment is
how you pray for her to one day know
this goodness
this salvation

hoisting your elbow up
they invite you to stand

peering about
you see
gathering has enclosed spaces
surrounding wooden offerings

in the air above
the orb is overwhelming
calmly thrashing blaze
jutting into strips
connecting atop wicks below

the child reaches out
with idle hand

firmly clutching the hand
holding your candle
mirroring their action
you extend your free palm to neighbor candle

soon web below
replicates one above
bound by flesh
joined by light
united by goodness

for a moment
all remain inert
until
as one body
step inward
constituting an indescribable explosion
engulfed by cylinder of unbroken light
big bang
divinum lumen
a new universe takes shape
one charged by genuine goodness

collective presence here
among the treetops
flickering as one

across a distant vale
a cloth extended above a shoreline
feels the pull of a heavy weight

as a meager
but tremendous
tear

lengthens

attainment of solidarity

golden incandescence
shimmers throughout the chamber

vermeil accents
growing radiance
supernova
contained in a cosmos
apart
yet one with the heavens you know

when you burn
you must burn together
ignited as one flame
singular dance of suffering
made bearable by knowing the pain as one

this
dearest one

is true humanity

an entity
inhabiting a diminutive planet
meant to function as a single organism
to grow
develop
outstretch itself
maturing into a multicellular body
one which nourishes
every atom within its form

humanity
was never meant to exist in many bodies
but to exist as one body
far different realities

goodness incarnate

such is the foundation of pure solidarity
when circles
surrounding greater center
thicken
solidify

tangible

observable
touched
felt

when unity exists
one looks upon others
seeing a reflection of their own
yet
dually the life of another

complete introspection
only finds fulfillment
when you are no longer material
but fluid
examined by how you mold
into the being
of standing together

left with no more
than spirit core

hollow
but full

without
with
all

perhaps the most difficult aspect of living
is the simple act of extending your arms

inviting a world
which may impale you
or embrace you

nevertheless
healing shall certainly not evince
without ones courageous enough
to submit

surrender

placing personal security
beneath the possibility of building something far greater

holiness in human bond

you see
dear one
it is never enough to revere prophetic voices
or even conclusive evidence
without following in their footsteps

you may be rejected
crucified
banished
invalidated

but take heart

for one day
when all have ventured the Void
peace
goodness
will finally know life

to build such a possibility
beware
cohesion is not constant
when formulated in times of sudden turmoil
or when many are speaking

nay
it is strongest
ingested every morning
prayed upon every evening

quickly constructed unity
or any shaped on virtues
other than goodness
love
will know the wrath of time

they will fail

never truly projected
for communal continuation
so multiply
fertilize
cultivate your goodness
goodness of all
but do so
with methodical remedy
assembled for longevity
intended to succeed
strength in authentic number

above all
recognize when solidarity
demands evolution
if more seek addition
intersectionality
healthier base
validated foundation

for
one can not rise from the ashes
unless there was first
a flame to burn

divine understanding
only comes when one humbles themself

epitome of wisdom
is found solely by offering oneself up
for the veneration of those alongside you

human dignity

defined by knowing yourself
and how one enriches
the humanity you are connected with

standing in unblemished unity
among all who breathe with you
all who onced breathed
all who one day will

for this
is the purest knowledge
one can ever know

meditate on this notion
as you allow your body to melt
further into thickening warmth

lose hold
separate cognition
morph into one being
with those here
those beyond
and those within you

absorb the divinity that is solidarity

an echo

deep from unseen bellies
within this great cavern

angelic reverberation
soothing rumble
breathes
into brumous atmosphere
serene stillness

hush

now

dissolve into blissful oblivion

Final Generations

upon acceptance of unity

one shall breathe the knowledge

of pure divinity

lament of Clemens

such a wise man once wrote
of the one who fell
into the Void first

birthright of Halley purification
bartered with the world
to understand the Void

true erasure
of sin
malice

to hold all impurity
on one soul

condone hate manifest
subverting messages
denigrating lenses of love
into compasses of conflict
fear
blame

if evil knows only one form
no other being need claim responsibility
all darkness must have once source

yet
this is not so

shadow submits to no master
bears no singularity
incarnation of malice is not a bloodline
but a credence
instructed by those who believe it outside them

immorality is no being
but an energy

one which flows
seeps
spreads

epidemics of ignorance
arrogance
slaughtering souls
rotting flesh from the inside out
separating humanity from divinity
by dividing them amongst themselves

to understand divine truth
release the shackles of fear
dogmas of a supreme sinner

step back
pray for your spirit
to speak the language of love
full veneration of all energies
forgiveness and compassion
to be poured into the rivers which etch the earth

warmth be granted to all
regardless of decisions once made
there is a place in serenity for all souls
even those who have fallen farthest
for who are you
to construct scales for nefarious measure

instead
create a mural of redemption
erect bridges for all to cross

for the greatest seeds of goodness
grow where the ground seems most barren

faux fruit

senses return in adagio sequence
tingling your fingertips first
ensuing with wiggle of toes
straining of ankles
stretching of neck
movement gives way to sighs of relief
soul-case still intact

finally unfastening eyelids
you find yourself in a foreign setting
an aching in your eardrums
suggests you have scaled altitudes
or depths

regardless
a vast variation of position
has stuffed air into audio canals

upon arising
location becomes evident
ferried to a new place
outcrop of rock and dirt
balcony overlooking previous landscapes
indent of chamber frame

region for reflection
within a realm of contemplation
kindred kind of library tabletops
seats to investigate worlds apart
but one with where they are kept

opposite lofty dropoff
footpaths lead toward a tranquil copse
with no other direction to decide upon
enter the brush

fleeting forest
greets boundless pasture
soothing meadow
pulsating carpet of dandelions
bulbinellas
black dahlia
gypsophila
bend in the breeze

intermingled with floral bloom
stunning aggregates of mineral and age
amethyst geodes
striking their presence into the air

sky above
infinitely inert
heavens stained brilliant hues
falu
sapphire
coral
fulvous

sunrise and sunset
dawn and dusk
alpha and omega
simultaneously etched welkin splendor

behold

lea of cosmic radix
holy ground
dwelling of divine energies
origin of absolutes
nativity of an ancient wisdom

this region perceives no time
utopian balance of light and dark
each has a place
purpose within this celestial space

gently tucked
between boulder pair
swirling geyser gushes
heaving scarlet haze into the atmosphere

scattered about
thriving trees
sag with throbbing fruits

streams of purple fluid
arteries supplying the land with recycling nourishment
surge off into the horizon

for the first time
the Void has no boundaries
no crag fortifications
no chamber lining
unrestrictedly sprawling toward infinity

as with so many explanations in human consciousness
this prairie too has been given many titles

Heaven
Eden
Jannah
Canaan
Nirvana
Brahman
Elysium
Moral Absolute
Peace of Mind

here has provided explanation
for the first falls
original sins
dependent origination
exact moments when mortal kind went astray
failed a most sacred source

maybe it was divine disobedience
perchance one ingested a forbidden fruit
slaughtered an eternal relationship with divinity
ungrateful generations
continuing to begrudge a personable deity

but
these accusations
beautifully constructed metaphors
for a far deeper disconnection

one between two
you foremost know

you

and

yourself

believing one does not necessitate
venturing the Void
to know thyself

for you can not know your world
your worth
or even a moral absolute
until you know yourself
and in turn
you shall lose yourself

deducing you are a piece of a collective power
an energy that has known no time
known no constraints
except those imposed
upon itself
by those which it is collated

surely you will be ignorant of worlds
if you remain ignorant of yourself

who

are

you

are you good
are you empty

who says
you
them
who are they
do they know you
do you know you

where does your goodness
emptiness
your ness ness
come from

does it come from them
from you
both
how do you know

such profoundly complex inquiries
indeed

nearby
sounds of a clearing throat
warrant a desire to investigate

atop eroding stone
a figure is perched
only paces away

damnation's place

elderly fingers
carefully detach citrus armor
from a spurting orange

rhythmically dropping each shaving
accumulating near their feet
every piece brings the peeler closer
to anticipated consumption

final chunk torn off
reveals a plump sphere
chewing
nectar dribbles down their chin
outstretching a humble hand
they offer you a bite

thanking them
you accept their generosity
indulging a second morsel
before giving the fruit back

catching you almost off guard
the elder speaks
strange place is it not
confused
you counter
where
this rocky crest above the Void
with quite an intriguing view

chuckling
the elder shakes their head
no
the Void itself
a most curious mind palace indeed

still requiring more context
you inquire

mind palace
meaning this place is all mirage
a creatively conducted dream
I will soon awaken from

again
they sway their head

most certainly not
unlike a mind palace for a singular entity
this place is very much a collective memory

a tapestry if you will
documentation of all that ever has transpired
weavings of individual experience
materialize a vibrant fabric
reflecting awe and horror

pausing to swallow final slices
they simper
licking away sticky remnants from their fingertips
before continuing

I should know
years have elapsed during my time here
many ventures I have undergone
each of my walkings on this path
brings an unbeknownst epiphany

you as well
have been here before
we all have
whether we realized or were unaware
an experience of the universal condition
so to speak

baffled
you respond

absurd
how can this be so
my perception of this place
has not been recognizable to me
I truly do not recall
wandering this road previously

for the first time
they nod in agreement

of course
the Void is not
a conventional thoroughfare
how could it be

an ever transfiguring being
placating distinct significances to each wayfarer

moreover
morphing for every specific journey they take
never presenting similarly as earlier renditions
for there is always new knowledge brought in
converted wisdom to egress with

pondering what has been spoken
you sit in silence
their analysis fascinating
though seemingly inconclusive

surely there are ludicrous aspects
to this likely senile person
however
they articulate with unwaivering proficiency

who must they be
in order to acquire such finite comprehension
of this befuddling place

though curiosity lingers
you refrain from prying
for the sake of decorum
considering you may have been acquainted
if you have frequently visited
nonetheless forgotten

seeking to adjust the conversation
you pose a query

is there a principal reasoning for the Void then
a coveted intelligence
patiently awaiting observance
by anyone in particular

a warm grin
spreads across wrinkling skin

on the contrary
the Void is the embodiment
of eternal searching

there are always questions to be contemplated
healing needing to be performed

quite extraordinary is it not
a place of such possibility and beauty
although plagued with destruction for periods
unfailingly finding rebirth

divine dance
with terrifying tempos
curing melodies

poetic inscription of cosmic relevance
perfect resemblance to the beings it imitates

a mosaic mirroring
every evolving cosmos in existence

captivated by plethoras
of insight being presented
you fixate on the elder's eyes
eager to know all they have witnessed
considerable amounts
no doubt

still interested in who they are
though mindfully regarding
previous decisions not to probe
you cleverly disguise the question
in an undetectable manner

indulge me this
if you will

why have you been commissioned
to venture the Void
it is evident you have no need to learn more
indisputably
you maintain a firm grasp on the meaning of this pathway
what benefit does this place serve for you exactly

lagging pause
worries you
may have crossed an offensive threshold

sighing deep
from pit of lung dwelling
the elder uneasily scratches their shoulders
discerning how to respond

anxiously they reach into their right pant pocket
fumbling to retrieve a small package
clear film coating
lid flipped
uncovers a handful of delicately rolled
tobacco-stuffed cylinders

plucking a cigarette from among its peers
they extend the box to you

flustered
though tempting after recent hardships
you decline their offer

appearing almost hurt
they promptly shrug
before withdrawing a lighter
from their left pocket
flicking flame into life

tenderly lifting the flickering to the edge of paper tips
like a soothing peck from a long-neglected lover

after drawing a few drags
puffing chemical rings out pursed lips
cradle their jaw upon bare palm
they speak

when you were a child
did you investigate fairytales

archetypes fed to you like fluffy white bread
always a terrible villain to be slain
stereotypes surviving on perpetuation

embedded morals
relaying abstractions of good
and inadvertently evil

perplexed
as to the importance
of such a question
you slightly nod
clearly puzzled

however
you feasibly grew to understand
women do not require constant saving
people of color are much more than minor characters
exclusively prescribed to cook
clean
tempt
or submit to a master

differences of the normalities
are not meant to be demonized
but respected
venerated

evil knows no body
no originating nationality
goodness is not always on a white horse

and hopefully
you saw the epidemic of manipulated morality
engineered as propaganda
deeming darkness as always unforgivable

but
villains are beings as well
deserving of dignity as are heroes

halting
with a suggestively melodramatic tinge
to inhale another whiff

gently tapping filter
excess ash tumbles to the ground
clearing their throat with a subtle wheeze
peering around as if expecting company

then resuming

it can be quite a lonely existence
being perceived a villain

heightened attention takes hold
perking your posture
to lean closer
you coax the statement on

oh
a villain
where did you receive such a title
what could you have done to deserve its connotation

sorrow escapes elder eyes
wiping away the tears
as more replace the formers

I made a grave mistake
committed highest crimes
against communal tranquility

I believed I could obtain an enlightened status
without humbling myself to knowing the Void

I did not require introspection
nor wisdom which comes from this pathway

for this
I was forced to witness the Void
the first blunder in cosmic remembrance
I surmised I did not need to enrich myself
and in turn
venerate my neighbors

in the beginning
I was full of such contempt
allowing arrogance to dictate my actions

attempting to seduce others to disavow self-awareness
disregard the importance of aiding
all in finding themselves as well

mistaken to think
a world could thrive
without knowing itself
truly knowing who it is
and valuing each who breathe within it

realization of who this must be
sends shock through your veins

Eve?
Adam?

a slight titter
as if they have been asked the very same
many times before

alas no

history has remembered me in various ways
given me countless names
a perpetual villain

I do not know what you understand me to be
but I have been called

pāpa
three poisons
chaos
immorality
ignorance
destruction
lucifer
iblis
devil
satan

paradise's face

an abrupt voice from behind
startles you

have you been smoking again

rotating
you gaze upon a new figure

as with the first
this individual exudes immeasurable age

their eyes
deep indigo
appear violet
hints of splattered silver slivers
glisten out from irises center
as though the sun had a twin
one forged by iodine gases instead of hydrogen

upon their shoulders
rests a flowing robe
cascading to their feet
mirroring eternal beats of ocean waves
lavish and limpid
free of impurities

from within the cloak lining
two hands
one contains no more than a ring
twisting round the fourth finger
whilst the second
grasps the neck of a mahogany instrument

child of strings family
cousin to violin
circularly constructed
cords worn and weathered

imprinted by fingers of one
who now holds its frame

returning your stare
upon their face
you wait for them to speak once more

I too remember
a time when I felt volition eluded me
watching events beyond
humanity's appetite for destruction
such a painful picture indeed
left with nothing but a vice and the hope they would learn
yet I found
smoking to cause such an increase in my anxiousness
thus I found this to utilize

gesturing to the instrument
they arch their elbow
elevating the object to a position of reverence

the first figure chuckles
drawing another helping of smoke
before responding

you know the greatest
I have never been one inclined to modes of practical comfort
alas there is always tomorrow to confront my demons

setting the instrument upon a near boulder
they gently tuck their robe trailing behind
and sit down

true
but tomorrow is only the extension of today
and today is merely the lagging dawn of the very first
so you know as well as I
that to look upon tomorrow
means you gaze upon today

scoffing
in a playful manner
the smoker admits defeat
raising their hands up
nodding in agreement
before taking a new inhale

silence returns
amongst your triad
now faced with another question
last time it was spoken
you received an unanticipated answer
eventually
you decide to refrain for now

after a time
newcomer vocalizes

after all this
how is your heart
do you feel empty

mind unsure
exhausted but coherent
you digest their words
discerning adequate description
of what you are enduring

sensing your struggle
they rephrase

what about this
do you feel full

reversing the statement
compels a far effortless answer

well yes
very much so

motioning for continuance
without breaking eye contact
they add

with what

articulation transfixes you
shamefully sulking
lowering your face
for you realize
you do not know

as a loving mentor
looks upon a perplexed pupil
observing nagging difficulty
in formulating a response
they beguile with sentences

instead
let me ask you this

are you aware
of undefined aftermaths
gushing through you

sentiments unfamiliar
aches unfelt prior
anguish actualized
but unmarked body
you still hold

surely
you recognize
you are encountering
plethoras of new realities
unbeknownst before
existent but unknown to you
your sanity is attempting to process

entities without names
emotions without designations

pausing
making sure you agree with their assertions
elicits a nod of approval from you
as they continue

these reactions
interpretations and reevaluations
are quite common among those before you

furtherly interested
you question

others have been here
others have known this bafflement

nodding
they expand on your query

of course
we sent them all

journeyed the Void they did
returned to the humanity
they left apart

to shepherd
to speak
a most fundamental truth

the instruction of goodness
fullness
divine solidarity

now too
we send you

your curiosity
overly prodded
surely they are baiting you
to ask what you seek

mustering confidence
unshackling disbelief
disregarding potential embarrassment
from incorrect hypotheses

redistributing how your frame slumps
projected chest
bones cackle
popping air pockets
snuggled between ligaments
you probe

are you God

inquisitively
they gaze into your eyes
their own
brimming with an emotion
you can not quite define

instead of answering
they respond with an
unexpected query of their own

may I play a song for you

taken aback
by their asking permission
of anything from you
awkwardly
indicate your approval

with permission granted
the elder
prepares their instrument
as they stand
you notice a detail
obscured previously

their cloak
is torn

sizable amount
absent presence
unevenly striped
frayed edges
as if forcibly removed

again an inquiry
for another time

as the elder
begins to serenade

upon thrumming of first chord
tremors
absorb into your body
melting through your pores
overwhelmingly
calm

upon the ground
grass blades
extend up
contort as do the notes
emulating a vibrational wave
as though natural order
moves to this very hymn

euphoric beginning
quickly transitions
melancholy mourning
tones turn violent
elder fingers trickle blood
strings gash into their skin

even for them
this song is painful to bear

music becomes you
is you
there is no detaching
your cognition
from the tempo around you
sound commands your body
heartbeats
rise
fall
level out
flatline

last note
fades with unquestionable force
elongated ebb
humbly triumphant
observation of a distant moment

when harmony
no longer needs an instrument
to be invoked

under their feet
grass once green
sags beneath brittle brown weight

centuries-old companions

relinquishing hold of their instrument
the elder lays the device
upon the boulder once more
wiping a sorrow-filled tear
from their eyes
they whisper

interpretation
is the oldest form of recognition

seeking an adequate absolute
which is only found in journeying the Void

as you have learned
this place
the energies
peoples
who manifest within
are all invoked with revolving names

such are beautiful products of language
culture
location
time

it is only plausible then
to understand
though the Void
those here
do not interiorly change
our exteriors are ever-morphing

therefore
here is my most honest
answer

let some say Yahweh

when I burned before Moses
he was a quiet man
Zipporah held him tighter
until he
took up the staff
walked with his people
led them from their bonds

exemplars
cast down
mountaintop transference
tablets may crack
eroded by winds of change
but true goodness
shall remain

let some say God

for when we sent Jesus
he listened

holding the hand of Mary
he grew in dust and sand
stumbled upon a road
older than the guillotine
slaughtered he was
trying to tell the world
the Void was existent

it was beckoning
is evident
humanity's redemption
revealed in the most obvious fashion
though remaining ignored
love above all

let some say Allah

for when Muhammad knelt
I was there
Hira could not contain
such rhythmic song
verses demanded transcription

Khadijah sanctified
he preached on corners
spoke of denouncing ignorance
tread the Void
know who you are
banished
migration began
as those before him
sealment of Abrahamic lineage

let some say Science

paradigms
composing physical Voids
natural order
absolute ever-evolving

Lemaître
witnessed initial illumination
Franklin
photographed eternally expanding helices
Fibonacci
saw the pyre spiraled clearing
Einstein
exposed structure of the Void
Euclid
mapped the path you now stand upon
countless others
examined quantified aspects of the Void

let some say deities

many of those here
have been witnessed
given names understood by observers

Trimurti
amaranthine triad
destruction
creation
continuance
each region of the Void
personified

Great Spirits
divided among elements
properties incarnate
anatomical representations
sacred portrayals
of happenings on this plane

let some say energy

when Gautama came
sat silently among us

finding such power
in the personal journey
individual experience of the Void
seeing this as principle
bringing all into alignment
sole communal tranquility

liberated from Samsara
physical fades
communal radiance
in a darkening clearing

let some say morality

many
they come
searching after catastrophe
before a great revolution

our answers
they enshrine
in living documents
archives of old

not always pure
meanings lost
manipulated
until
descendants come
rewriting in mind
expecting to rebuild
and heal

let some not know

there is no shame
in acknowledging
a concept
a reality
that can not translate
for you

however
this is indication
you must continue searching
for no answer
is only a state
preparing
for the grand wandering

taking a moment
to gather their breath
robe-wearer
mutes

fruit-eater
now interposes

you see
dearest child
pay no mind
to importance of what we are called

unlike human beings
differentiating names
does not disregard our journey
for we have journeyed the Void
our existence is horizontal
nothing loses meaning
when invoked differently

whereas humans
are vertical

there is but one
absolute title
which adequately invokes their truth
remember this

diversified deciphering of us
is our intention
continuance
varying relevance
if we had wanted it any other way
only one mind would exist

the Void
would need not be

what all are comprehending
primordial entities
are two realities

one of which
I unfortunately epitomized

emptiness

the lacking of goodness
what all shall strive from
is not evilness
nay
it is emptiness

existing
is but a circle
a most delicate sphere

true goodness
complete oneness
as you experienced out in the clearing
comes only when the circle is firmly solidified

anything less
than the solidarity of fulfillment
the production of goodness
is only an unjoined circle

until the moment
when the final piece
of circumference
is placed

searching
unactualized
empty

transitioning notions
constitutes a new speaker
as the robe-wearer speaks again

undeniably
the greatest detriment
to the progression of human collectiveness
is oppression guised as morality

then one must wonder
what is moral
what is goodness

the answer to all this
unnecessary grief
is actually quite rudimentary

do not
distance yourself from those
who interpret differently
engage them
learn of their life
value their struggles

do you tear down other personhoods
only to placate your own
do not entertain hate
in any form

genuine goodness
unvarnished morality
does not destroy
but dignifies

it is not loud
but soft
does not harm
but harmonizes

it is a meek voice
calling out in the darkness

it is unassuming
for it assumes nothing of another
allows all voices to speak
whether they are concurring
or differing

it is intersectional
consecrates every being
unhinged on anything but
humanness most venerated

so
dearest child
let goodness be your guide
your morality
and you shall reveal wonders
unimagined

every moment
will reflect your experiences in the clearing
upon the guillotine
in the presence of all
for the remainder of Voids
which beckon unto you

conclusion of explanations
leaves you lost in thought
conceptualizing how you
can live a life in accordance with goodness

onerous roads before you
likely more arduous than this Void
for the pathway toward goodness
has never been one of comfort
it demands sincerest resolve

one question
remains unspoken
details noticed before their song
a torn cloak

you would regret
not garnering the knowledge
why this is so

gently you speak

may I ask
why you wear a shredded robe

running their fingertips
along cloth seams
they contact place where tear begins
bringing the empty space forward
outstretching their arm
giving enormity full due
as they reply

long ago
a moment
I have never forgotten
when the first act of emptiness
transpired
my wrappings were sliced
by one I most loved

next to them
the first elder
lowers their head
though not in shame
but reverence
for when knowledge is obtained
realizations of wrongdoings
chagrin can be eliminated

you have witnessed
my missing piece
far off
above a distant shoreline
recording emptiness occurring
throughout the universe
it shall remain there
for even goodness
was once empty
and goodness
is merely the fulfillment
of any aching emptiness

keep the ruins
construct from there
for the past
is the greatest of pedagogues

contemplating answer given
remembering the cloth
somewhere in the Void
though not much time is allotted
for again they speak

we would like to show you
a place
where your goodness
is buried

sown spiritual maxims
spurts of knowledge
levied with rooting grip
cultivating
reaping mind

rising
both figures
invite you to follow

a gated garden

striding in tow
escorts shepherd you
through flowing fields

halting before a most gorgeous gate
silver rods swirl
wispy like smoke
form an awing partition

your guides turn and face you
as though waiting for indication

unsure
you remain still

smiling
one of the pair speaks

only you
can open this gate child

skepticism floods your face
though you step forward
noticing no keyhole
no method to open
you stand scrutinizing the entrance

from behind
the other presence speaks

lay your hands upon the surface

heeding advice given
you present open palms to the structure
upon contact
silver rods sizzle
shimmering as they dissolve into the ground

now exposed
internal organs
flowers
saplings
leaves
move to a luminescent rhythm

conductor of this symphony
lies center
upon scarlet ground

from roots
pulsation sent out
echoing through the surrounding structures
tempo of curious palette
commanded by a humble tree
resting at focal location

similar to a demon
slain moments ago
trunk is one of mirage

near the base
a young child dances
with an old woman
spinning to the beat
of inaudible instruments
you know this woman
you know this child

hovering above familial duo
the same child sits
perched between palms
not yet callused
a book
glee gambols across young pupils
as the story unfurls like sorcery
cast from another's pencil tip

further up
the child has begun to change
age splattered across their face
intermingled with solemn
as they stand above a lowering casket
burying one you loved most dearly

nearing convergence
of limb and trunk
image of you holding a carton
cardboard box
you are moving perhaps
leaving
returning
arriving
somewhere of significance to you

into the branches
portrait of you on bended knee
weeping
an ending has occurred
friendship
relationship
something of significance to you

mid branches
display you among a blessed gathering
circled within a clearing

shuttering through top branches
eerie duplication
you
stand
peering forward
with two shapes behind

the tree recalls your life
even now

breaking the noiselessness
the latter figure speaks

this is your garden
dear child

anchor of your soul
spiritual bedrock
cornerstone of consciousness

you have always known this garden
returning in times of trouble
contemplating that which consumes you
disturbances filtering through your mind
deciphering courses of action
counsel when called upon
forged with frontal lobe

here
is home to your conscience
eternal birthplace
immortal tomb

the very essence of you
built this space
builds this space

centered
you find your tree
record of knowledge
ode to your own growing
thirstful for knowledge
awaiting the comprehensions
found as you exist among the universe
fertile by your command
most sacred organ
functioning in the space between seen
and unseen

now
the second figure interjects

this garden
is a holy place indeed
wander about
explore the space you call home

leaving the pair
you head off
on your own

such wonderment
growing around you
vigorous shades
surge
circulating and descending

blossoms
similar to those
which breezes swayed
in your past

dangling
favorite fruits
preferred palates
ooze with ripeness

a small stream
glistens
rushing against
onyx pebbles

investigation terminates
as abruptly
you find yourself
standing before the mighty tree

the holy book

scrutinizing closer
you observe an odd occurrence
riddling the trunk

entire chunks of bark have been stripped away
if this was not strange enough
each space of absence
perfectly symmetrical sheets
cavities intentionally embossed
sheets of sorts
perhaps meant for a most peculiar binding

with anxious inquiry on your tongue
you face your companions

is the tree sick

smiling upon your genuine concern
the figure holding an instrument responds

no dearest one
the tree does not know an ailment of any kind
what you gaze upon now
is the remanence of labor before this time
carried out by the very one before me

by thine own hands
has the tree known this sculpting

not with enmity
have you performed these deeds
on the contrary
each marking
pays tribute to pages past
those already written

confused once more
apprehension becomes you
you press further

for what reason
did I strip the tree so

ripples of gentle warmth
caress their face

to construct
a masterpiece

come
we shall show you

as the figures guide you
nearer to the tree

time dissolves
movement is not slow
though it is not rapid
movement itself
ceases for a moment

it is of no importance
for here
at foot of this growth
a holiness shall be revealed
one time
could never contain

merely you
the pair you travel with
and events about to occur
a moment beyond time

there at base
upon the ground
sits a simple rectangular chest

protected within
instruments gathered
for ceremony nigh

a screen
mahogany frame
mesh-stretched interior

a solid board
equal in size to the screen

finally
exposed bottom
half full of crystal-clear water
provide ingredients
necessary to convert pulp to page

fracturing quietness
the figure
deemed emptiness manifest
speaks

behold
young child
the holy book
canon of your thoughts
transcription of your wanderings
record of your life journey
fashioned from the very tree sustaining your spirit
it is one with your memory
for it is the byproduct of its most intimate happenings

each venture of the Void
results in an addition to this sanctified collection
some journeys produce chapters
others pages
still fewer
assemble mere sentences
but no matter

your life is not complete
until the binding brims with material
only then is your book prepared to be placed
within the Great Garden

rested amongst all others

becoming the tree of life
all have a chapter
contained within the expanding
eternal
narrative

now go
go unto this bole
strip your psyche
bend and blend its body
into a page fit for recordance

minding direction
you saunter
unto the thick trunk
now as close
as one can be
without becoming the tree itself
you evaluate slightest features

though presenting
as solid form
the tree
is a mighty composition
miniscule cells
contained within each
modest nucleus
flashes every breath
you have taken

every moment
even ones presumed insignificant

a celebration
a nighttime walk
laughing
tear shed
darknesses
bright lights
each echoing
in the very units
of your living memory

gently lifting your hand
cupping your palm
you carefully scrape a collection of the surface
like fresh snow
specks accumulate
congealing
into purple mush

deliberate
handling with care
you transfer the paste
into the open chest below

heavily drifting
sinking
spreading through water
wine-colored cloud

mixture curdles
tenderly you submerge your hands
twisting fingers
breaking apart clumps
evenly thinning
labored to desired consistency

once texture intended
is reached
you retrieve
screen and board from the floor
positioning the plank next to you
you heave mounted mesh up
dunking into swirling concoction

after pausing
you delve in
withdrawing webbed device
now coated in layers of pulp

meticulously moving
you bring the mesh
dripping excess water
over to the resting board

setting soaked rectangle down
you pick up clean slab
aligning the pair
you press
hovering board
into the mush
murky water dribbles from corners

compressing with flat palms
you continue to excrete liquid
binding fibers into one

flipping wooden couple
evening pressure
designs smooth paper

once the process
no longer expels moisture
you raise the screening

beneath
firmly packed onto harder material
organic page
begging for ink
to glaze its body

prudently you peel
the sheet from its place
slow and decisive
for if hurried or careless
the newborn will surely tear

fully detached
the strip must dry
next to you
overhanging branch
provides a perfect place

draping an edge
over each arm
you present the lamina to the branch
gracefully allowing it to arch
bending across the timber limb

with no more actions
than awaiting page to dehydrate
you turn your eyes
consciousness
back to the elders
who have been sitting nearby
observing with anticipation

peering toward
product of your travail
the musician approvingly declares

splendid artwork

beloved one
you have made an exceptional piece
worthy of your expanding volume

thanking them for their flattery
you join their sedentary place
only a few paces away

beside you now
the smoke-breather reaches
once more
into their pocket
revealing a little utensil
brimming with ink
written lover

soon
you shall need this

extending your gratitude
you grip the apparatus
laying it on the ground

looking to their partner
they both nod

like a lullaby slathered in honey
or a prayer
dipped in soft chocolate
the elder clothed in purple
whispers

it is time

standing
both figures stretch their limbs
inviting you as well

upon straightening
one of them joyfully enunciates

know we
see you
validate you
believe in you
continue seeking the goodness
give it life
keep it always on your tongue
entwined in your fingertips
embedded in your veins
and soon
we shall meet again

together
they embrace you
as an unbroken trio
becomes one

releasing their holds
they both lean in
kissing each of your cheeks
before stepping backward

with a final farewell
for now
the pair extend one arm each
locking themself with the other
they turn
speaking inaudibly
sharing a friendly laughter
as they depart from view

now alone
just you and your thoughts
you can concentrate

returning to the crisping page
you find it hardened
ready to be written upon

stooping over
you clutch the small scribbler
stripping branch of its cover
you look for a place to compose

upon the surface
of self-made paper
you must pour the experiences
witnessing
events of this Void
unwavering
precise
let it all go
dear one

upon this page
write

with each word written
paper begins to crack
periodic chunks
fall away
absorbing into tree roots
every trickling intake
illuminates the garden further

keep penning
until nothing remains unauthored

tell the tale

of this Void

everlasting perennial

the strongest structures
endure

not
built upon sand
rock
even of the earth

but sown in the fertile soil of a soul

sanctuary never vacant
always accepting company
regardless of creed
without color constructs
unasking of offertory
practicing unspoken prayer
praise despite pasts

the heaven you search for
is contained with you
generations before you
built your bones
essence of continued human holiness
passed down
through humble lumber bloodline

fascinating
how many Voids involve a wooden vessel

burning bush
ark of gopher planks
cross
Bodhi Tree
Bahubali thighs
Prophet's Tree
pencil of the thinkers
brush of the creators

surely these seedlings
are not the source of divine awareness
rather they mirror the obtaining of such knowledge

perhaps
proximity to this ancient lifesource
direct cycle of breathing
provides one deeper thoughts
ancestors
humans have forgotten how to acknowledge

trees
designed to reflect themselves
growing above
growing below
natural depiction of infinity

pulsating a primordial chorus

om
photosynthesis
ik onkar
holy spirit

epicenter of internal contemplation
birth in root and dirt
nestled beneath the shelter of much older relatives
here is where you shall find wisdom
as this tree grows with you
you grow with it

interwine your spine with bark bole
twisting upward
downward
stronghold of conviction
marked map of existence

never cease cultivation

it is imperative
you live a life nourishing your soul
but do so with the collective human soul in mind

build bridges
never barriers

hold the weeping
and weep with them

bandage the wounds of another
with strips of your own skin

stop the bullet
by blocking intended targets

open dialogues
never silence those you not agree with

end genocides
intellectual and physical

no longer gentrify cultures
erase lineages deemed archaic

selfishly seek thy purpose
to selflessly live for the greater

lay your essence down
without asking for anything in return

but beware
as you do this
do not fall into believing yourself to be a savior
this only negates the piety of purpose
all were born to be prophets
not for notoriety
but for humility before their neighbor

you see

humans
have an unprecedented ability
no other being on earth can perform
the acquirement of perpetual peace

coexistence is quite obtainable
but it shall take perseverance from all

it will not be in the wake of war
you will not find it on a battlefield

nor in the temples

it does not dwell in written works
nor in the hands of dignitaries

it is not buried in the earth
neither does it levitate in heavens above

you will find its roots in the mental woods
where trees and vegetation reign
whispering a primeval dogma

that all life
imprints the tapestry of time
planted with a purpose
only understood through inspecting the Void

there is no dignity
in diminishing the purpose of another

there is no holiness
in holding few to positions of value

there is no divinity
in desecrating the heartbeat of humanity

there shall be no survival
if you do not submit yourselves to one another

bound by love
sealed with solidarity
marching together into the remainder of history

that will be the moment
when humanity reclaims the right to hope themselves redeemable
salvation through sincere sanctity of each

a society constructed upon pillars of anger
division
hate
emptiness
shall never know prosperity

if all of humanity
venerated their tree
visiting often
contemplating the heaviest of circumstances
image the garden which would know life
forest of unfailing goodness

all who have ever known existence
divine perennials
sown by cosmic ordination
stewarded by their own hands
grown without restriction of time

for vessels of flesh expire
but timberland of vitality
infinite paradigm rooted in universal avail
shall not know the conditions of dissolution

this is the divine truth
veneration is the highest of virtues
to truly know deific wisdom

you must begin with valuing that which is created
by the very epicenter of galactic glory
for all is lingering dust
scattered cosmic organisms

humans are not merely similar
no
all are byproducts of this ancient ash
embers of a primordial blaze
a moment of purity
forgotten by time

individual composition
reflected by anatomy
echoes planetary elements
constellational remnants infuse your air
bones beneath your skin
building blocks for a much greater narrative
spiritual significance exists within all things

so grow
grow with your tree
mirror lasting nourishment
sow barren ground
reap in times of harvest
remain resolute in eras of isolation

but never uproot another
for that deludes your purpose
your own thriving
the value of all

debates upon designation shall continue
humans reserve a need to name
but no matter
circular entities are undefinable
each radii valid by measure
equal distance from origin

this is the human narrative
dear child
one littered with horrendous misdeeds
desecration
denial
defamation
ruthless annihilation

but oblivion
is by your own design
only by own decisions
can anything truly cease

even then
ceasing
is a facade

truly transformations
starting anew

the essence of humanity
very definition of the Void
contained within five humble syllables

to begin again

but to begin
does not hinge upon elimination
embedded in glorious transference
combustion of continuums

one trunk
many branches
one soul
many bodies
one rhythm
many dances

one Void
many ventures

you see
dearest one
you are everlasting growths
scattered through time
to be

as one

one beginning
one continuation

until the final drum shall beat
the Void folding into itself
circle concaving to center

signaling the redemption of humankind
must you continue searching

peeling into yourself
examining the very bonds that bind you
to those outside you
those inside you

until that moment
journey back
into the Void
each moment
of each sun cycle

venerating the wanderings
all shall face
though distinct

it is one

seal and heal

this journey of the Void
hastily nears completion

though as by design
you will return many times over
each expedition

witness
experience
learn

before you depart
returning to dimensions you left
take a moment

gaze below
from this meadow
draped on cliffs above
perfectly spread like butter
totality of your odyssey unfolded

recent places
a boulder
decaying fruit peels
litter the base
where you spoke with ancient energies

enshrouding the rocks
luscious treetops
sway an embellished movement
waves of verdant and mahogany
awkwardly off-centered
circular clearing punctures through the green mass
contained within
brilliantly gleaming structure of twigs and symbols
monument to a communal redemption

coruscating tapers
continual flames
held by single grasps
inscribing an eternal unity
purity of human spirituality
only found in burning as one

remnants of a lavish festival
originating from many objects
victories over elegiac guilts

visually tracing up the forest
eyes rest upon a gravel road
veining out from canopy cover
leading to a curious heap of remains
atop the trail
once guarded by a most ferocious evil
unbarred passage reigns

towering over destruction sites
indented sierra
through which a tunnel was navigated
linking your crossing
with other sides

inverse valley from that of the pyre
mist mingling pit rests
residue of erroneous gatherings
convention of misguided prudence

idol of wood and steel
splintered
toppled to depths below
nevermore bestowing ostracism
enrichment defiled as regulation

continuing past a small grove
eerie tapestry

flows in unrolling breeze
unfortunately this wound on human inheritance
remains
only when all experience the Void
will this lasting mark fully unravel

strides away
sand converges with waterway
river winding upward
far distance
shoreline ebbs into base of a monstrous mound

structure of worship
graveyard resting beneath
where more may be left
though no longer forsaken

outside metal fenceline
descending street
leads past buildings
childhood homes
reminiscence withering into graceful dust

furthest from view
at tip of visual horizon
a solemn silhouette
scarcely distinguishable
holding a miniscule match

fading glow
marker of journey beginnings
nervous to venture forward

mirror of one
quickly becoming a new memory
safeguarding a genesis
now resolution revelation

observe

wreckage
spectres
voices
rejuvenation

do not convince yourself
this entire chamber is not worthy of reverence
ruins grow weeds
water erodes cobble paths
time continues crumbling framework

however
take heart
leave the past as a place to visit
find solace in building somewhere new
not spiting the ruins
but letting them embody their importance

hold them close
but cherish them enough
to let them go

for there will always be Voids to travel
ruins to venerate
roads to walk
knowledge to obtain

but in this moment

breathe out
breathe in

it is time

for this Void
no longer beckons

departing the fall

thgir

u thgir thgir
p
u thgir thgir thgir
p
u thgir thgir
p
u thgir
p u
left left left p
u
left left left left p
u
p
n n n n n n u
w w w w w w p
o o o o o o
d d d d d d

departure from the Void
is a disorienting process
directions unknown
rapidly spinning
or possibly
dropping deeper
no rising
falling up perhaps

no matter
for your feet make contact with pavement

rubbing your eyes
irritated by blast of sudden brightness
you find yourself before a familiar structure

overhead
steady flurries cascade
from sagging clouds
powdering the ground a pleasant alabaster

gently snuggled between two highrises
a small coffeehouse
refurbished neon sign
flashes a welcoming message

through storefront window
people bustle around the warm interior

out here
on the street
people meander about
bundled up against chilly winds
couples holding hands
children laughing
steamy cocoa nestled in their mitts

you wonder if they too have ventured the Void

shrill honking approaches
you notice you are stationary in the road
waving apologies at oncoming traffic
you quickly glide to the sidewalk
finding yourself in front of the coffee shop

open the door
surely it is a hearth
compared to this frigid weather
furthermore
you could entertain a drink

reflections on the promised land

dim lightning
provides an aesthetic ambiance

in the far corner
a small
round table
snuggles worn chairs

settling down
you remove your coat
which materialized moments ago
out in the cold

what would you like to drink?

there is water
coffee
cocoa?
what about a soda?
warm milk?
tea with honey?

a server approaches
scribbles shorthand of your requested order
before swiftly returning behind swinging doors

amidst muddled murmuring from fellow patrons
an inaudible presence of sanctity
surrounds this space

having spent unmeasurable amounts
in a realm far different
from current location
constructs of time are disorienting

it will take awhile
for you to readjust
being among the familiar

you find yourself
linger on watching
a young child
sitting with their parents
sipping a fizzing drink
wondering what pain they might know
if they are aware
of unforgiving realities all around them

you look upon their parents
pondering if they will prepare their child
to face forthcoming anguish

will they too
hold onto a casket
run atop an impenetrable river
fruitlessly search for answers
only the Void can teach

gathering your thoughts
you return focus to yourself
noticing for the first time
how rewarding sitting feels
no pressing need to continue walking
moving
allowed an uninterrupted moment
to rest
reveling in sense of physical release

though you relax
even now
you are actualizing the Void

once you venture in
you evermore see reflections within the world

it is important to know
the journey itself
does not conclude

Exodus
Calvary
Hijrah
Middle Way
Paths to Liberation
Faith
Morality
Axons

always meeting you
in the most unlikely of moments

as circumference is traveled

until the circle collapses inward

this is the way of the enlightened
those who invoke
deep significance unto each moment
every human interaction
always examining their universe
through the lenses
of their Voids
but recognizing
the Voids of others
are also present

this meager coffee shop
a place where individuals
intersect
meeting to rekindle lagging connections
stumble upon new friendships
a perfect place
to inspect the Void
colliding amongst mismatched strangers

those who sit
sprawled out
probing their minds
to create
dissent
formulate experimental ideas
construct novel writings

existing apart from the hurried world
beyond glass windows
but a part of those beyond
just in a space of constant viewing

emerging from behind swinging doors
the server
hoists a tray
carrying your order

tenderly setting your drink
in the space between your arms
they ask if you need anything else

graciously you say not currently
but you pause
thinking back
to the clearing in a woods
where human solidarity hinges

you inquire
what their name is

seeming confused
though smiling
they chuckle for a moment
before responding

Aurora

thanking them
you look down to your cup
when you notice they must have made a mistake

nothing was brought for me

before you wave them down
asking them to take my order
look at me

can you see me?

now bewildered
for I am nowhere to be seen
for a moment you worry
you have imagined this whole ordeal

but
dearest one
you knew
all along
who I was
did you not

you can always hear me
for I reside inside you
but only within the Void
can I separate to guide

as is the Void
those you met there
I am always with you

your conscience
soul
you
we are of the same my dearest one

apart from multiples of love
I give you
these parting words
before you call upon me again

the world
we are existing within
this very instant
is suffering

it is breaking
it is burning

and the only question worth asking

is what shall we do about it

as we go about
the remainder of our life

always remember

where
veneration is present
beauty can be built

if you ever seek to find me

you know what path I tend

you know where to search

until then

farwell

dearest messiah
ordinary prophet
savior of our soul
builder of our own
go forth
conquer the obstacles

of life
of death

in

apart

and of

the Void...

Most
Sincerely in Ink;

An afterword of the *Void*, its universal reprecussions, and how this journey is the cornerstone of instrospective altruism.

7.18.16

4:54 post meridiem

Dearest Companion,

The roadways of an artist's life bring a great deal of sadness, turmoil, and seemingly perpetual doubt. However, these strenuous paths concurrently gift artists introspection, awareness, and complete appreciation. Throughout the journey this collection has taken me on, I have experienced each of these attributes amidst countless of their peers.

This manuscript was painful, and I neglected it many times throughout its formative months. Witnessing the aftermath of social, political, and ethical events unfolding throughout the past year, made entering the Void each day even more demanding. After some time, I came to realize why this venture was so difficult to transcribe; I was not solely writing fiction, I was transcribing non-fiction, and such an epiphany was arduous to bear.

Many tribulations presented themselves while I formulated this delicate binding - not all of them were triumphed. In fact, many of the atrocities recollected are alive and fertile even now. It is my sincerest prayer that, as our culture progresses in the coming centuries, we come to truly discern these moments in humanity's legacy. Has the cloth's growth decreased, or has it increased momentum in its unfurling crusade?

This Void Beckons is not a work meant to critique a singular moral system, lifestyle, nor any specific religious or secular tradition. Nor does this journey propose an undisputable truth. Rather its purpose is a universal pilgrimage of introspection and communal unity, ultimately fusing the fruits of such a divine union. An individual who has not stepped into the Void can not obtain the idiosyncratic, yet collective, insight which comes from walking the way. This is the only truth worth knowing. This is the absolute; the Void exists, it beckons, and demands invocation.

Every revolution ignites with the visionaries, moreover the artists. As curators of culture, it is the artists' responsibility to mobilize, fashioning a manifestation of the social atmosphere at hand. As a collective human family, we have aspired to find a definitive absolute.

Religions, philosophies, nations, ideologies have been built upon ardently accurate notions. Where these institutions fail, art has the obligation to construct conducively. The fruits of artistic labor shall always be the antithesis of any problematic, institutional deficiency.

Radical goodness does not take precaution in vetting those "worthy" of reception; it does not prescribe to caring about worthiness. There is no crime, no sin, no immoral action which can erase the absolute truth of human dignity. The only way to know a true divinity, a god above, or a universal peace, is for us to all radically venerate one another; a process that begins in the unrestricted confines of the Void.

Upon the pathway journeyed by billions, travelers are presented with the trinity of realities. Each plane exists without the others, however their union is the Void. Only once joined, comprehended, and subsequently enacted by the observer, is the Void actualized. In order to fully appreciate, channel, and manifest the Void, we must recognize and understand the integral aspects of this primordial place.

Understanding that the Void is dually a magnificent metaphor, as well as a concrete representation of the human condition, allows us to apply countless narratives to the journey. This path is not merely our own, but the very plane human history has functioned upon since time immemorial. Upon this plane is where multitudes of prophets, religious leaders, creative minds, empirical questioners, deep thinkers, and every person has found themselves existing. We exist there. We exist here.

Authentic being is a pilgrimage through the continual processes of deduction and induction. To live an enlightened life, it must be a conscious one. The experience of the Void, and dually our everday living, presents us with recurrent opportunities to be conscious of the happenings around us. It is our responsibility as members of the human family to actively engage this state of consciousness, and challenge ourselves to live in constant accordance with the trinity of realities. Living otherwise is not only a grave disparity of human potential, but pretext for the cloth's lengthening. In order to learn how to live consciously, we must venture into the beckoning Void. Upon entering, we are immediately exposed to the first reality in the trinity. It is here where our journey commences.

....

You. *Cremations*

The primitive step in understanding your own mind is remembering you are your mind. Of the utmost importance is allowing yourself to strike the match and light your way forward, instead of denying the entire cosmoses; existence within you.

Upon invoking the Void, we are immediately presented with a reality only worthy of the title *Cremations*. The experience of self-journey and self-actualization must be a gorgeous blaze. We must step into the flame, eventually morphing into ash, to examine our most dissectable attributes.

Who are you at your complete core? Are you empty? Are you searching in the wrong places? Are you laboring without authentic cause? Are you good?

These ponderings are the backbone of a healthy, productive, and redeemable human future. When we examine ourselves, we are met with numerous Voids; and begin existing in both a world which mirrors the Void, and a world which is the manifestation of its tangible production. The moment these realities are indistinguishable, the human race has stepped into a collective conscious of true goodness.

The difficult question daringly becomes - what constitutes goodness? For answers, we must turn to the pathway recently walked. Experiencing the Void, we find that goodness is the byproduct of striving to decrease the gaping craters caused by emptiness. To know goodness, we must first know emptiness - undeniably the starting point for all.

Emptiness is familiar to us. It is comforting to not extend ourselves into positions of discomfort. To know goodness, we must first know ourselves and extend such discoveries outward - a daunting task. However, there shall never be hope for collective human goodness unless each is willing to disrupt the comfortable paradigms of emptiness, and lose all sense of ownership, in order to obtain goodness.

As asserted earlier, the Void is the consummation of three concrete realities. Both the concept of 'goodness', as well as the realities where the Void exists are manifested in spherical form. Moreover, the Void itself is a sphere. It is an uncontained continuation, that exists for eternity in all directions.

The preliminary reality, most intimately known to you, is the reality of 'You'. In the Void, existence as 'You' must come to a glorious end, for the obtainment of goodness demands you to lose yourself. Cremations is the Void's personal pathway. It is the section where you meet your most distant memories, the people you have left, the places you have built, and witness them crumble.

We all begin empty. In fact, we would not need the journey in the first place if we were not so. Below are diagrams representing an individual prior to experiencing the reality *Cremations*, and the individual afterward.

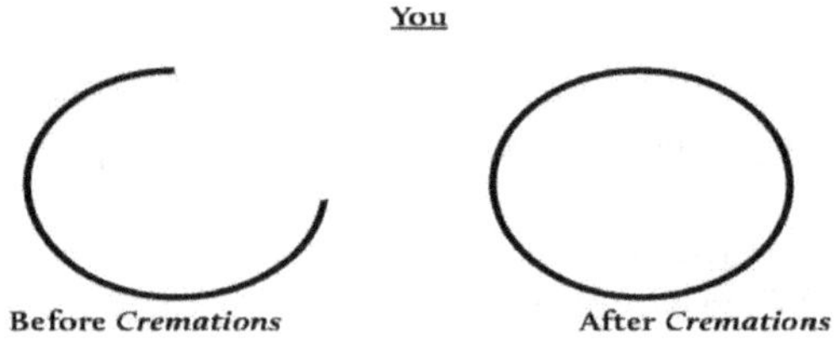

*for clarity, the diagrams are presented as circles.

As it is understood, any sphere that is not fully realized is empty. Until the sphere has come to complete circumference, it retains emptiness where the space is unjoined. So too is the functionality of goodness.

It is vital to note, that once the sphere is joined, the individual who has fulfilled the Void is not finished. Goodness is a continued struggle. It is not a stagnant destination but an eternity of spiral. While our existence is spherical, and closing the sphere is possible, the pathway taken is not a singular encounter. It does not end. It begins again.

To begin, we must light the flame, engulfing the vast darkness before us in radiance. Illumination heralds the commencement of the Void, beckoning us onward. Stepping into the mysterious and sacred space, we are met with the crumbling ruins of our own pasts. The memories remain looming, each a seemingly daunting presence to distant times. They gift us the prominent aspects of prior experiences, for if we want to know ourselves fully, we must know who we have been.

While present in the reality of *Cremations*, we witness the three obstacles that constrict our own progress toward goodness. These obstacles are personified and observed as we walk our way. These individuals show us what practices and archetypes cause a wanderer to lose their way, to stray from the path toward personal and communal goodness.

The first impediment to our journey is the presence of abandoned innocence. A child, one who reflects our own childhood figure, kneels alone in a desolate cemetery. They have been left to venture into adulthood without guidance or support from familial, social, or cultural ties. They are the abandoned soul; the perpetually waiting mind. Inert and unprogressive in their trek toward goodness, for they were never even shown what goodness was. They are the manifestation of loneliness, solitary suffering, and neglect in the formative years of one's life, illustrating the detriment pain can cause a searching soul. Departing from the child's confinement, we find ourselves in a potentially familiar structure - a house of worship, where a man has locked himself in a cycle of unproductive servitude.

The man observed within the deserted sanctuary is the embodiment of righteousness. He is the problematic belief that true goodness is merely a dogma, unpracticed outside the walls of a holy place. A hollow body, torturing themselves by believing they have praised incorrectly. Those who limit their searching for goodness to scriptures, to moral outlines, to the physicality of the world. Inadvertently, they live life, believing to be rooted in goodness, but only enacted from the comfort of their self-induced limitations. There is no observance of inclusion for the righteous. There is no invocation of intersectionality or further prodding into the spiritual binding fibers of the human family. There is only their soul, and the morality they invoke. They shall always search in the wrong place for answers only found in the discomfort beyond their righteousness. From the tower of perceived absolutes, the final figure is found in a state of persistent anguish.

Upon a mighty river's surface, we meet the tormented woman. She is the paragon of a soul existing in denial. Believing she has the power to change that which has already passed. She allows her ruins, her reality of self, to be haunted by the past. She denies the movement of self, the necessity of healing, instead she remains in a stagnant space, attempting to bring back what has gone; what has changed. It is the burden of those in denial to engage an unwinnable struggle, one without triumph. There is no end to the denier's journey, they will only find themselves in a spiral toward oblivion. There is no easing the pain of one who is sinking in denial, for denial is only broken by accepting the uncomfortable. To break the cycle, one must come to terms with the past as a place to value, but not exist within, for it is not a plane one can return to. As the Void is journeyed, as lives are lived, one must do so without the pervasive presence of inertia toward growth, righteousness, or denial to limit progression.

Leaving the trio of exemplified personal deterrents, one is brought before the most heinous mark on the human legacy. A grotesque cloth, unfolded by the decree of hasty malice. Before one can experience remnants of societal degradation, they must bear witness to the historical record. The cloth, as described in this collection, depicts merely a handful of atrocities sanctioned by human history, predominantly those transpired in the last few centuries. Countless volumes could, and must, be transcribed to adequately and accurately recollect the multitude of dignity deficiencies the human race has caused. It is imperative, while journeying the Void, and living daily life, one remembers and acknowledges the existence of the cloth, the tapestry of torment, and what it symbolizes.

Perhaps the pinnacle of the Void's first reality takes form at the base of a great pit. Witnessing modern examples of social and cultural oppression is imperative to finding issue with the problematic structures and practices in current society. With witness comes discontent. From discontent comes passion, and passion leads to desire for reform. It is only through witnessing and observing, not ignoring the horrendous deeds of humanity, will one come to demand change.

Before the guardians of the guillotine descend upon you, they showcase their vast, communal emptiness. Their destruction of human bodies, dignity, and worth by utilizing ignorance, discrimination, and bigotry goes unchallenged. Cultures, peoples, and identities are banished to positions deemed 'lesser', and above their gathering is the crown apparatus of emptiness - the guillotine. With the guillotine, you witness the removal of a woman's tongue. The crowd demands that she be stripped of her ability to claim vocal ownership of her autonomy, that she be unable to speak opposition to her own oppression. In this world, it is the legacy of oppressors to find strength in the perpetual silencing of those they believe beneath them. It is only once one has surmounted the most vile social degradation, can they find the strength to claim their self-sustaining comprehension of worthiness. It is through our own declaration of self, of identity, of worthiness, that allows us to fulfill our personhood.

Existing in a complete alignment of mind and body is the foundation of authentic personhood. In order to truly know who we are, how we can effectively enact our purpose in the world, and build a life of lasting goodness, we must lose ourselves. It is that most divine sacrifice, the selfless giving of one's self for the common good. This is the apogee of the personal Void: the personal death. As understood in the Void, death is merely where the sense of self ends and meets the collective human spirit.

The aspect of self, which is slaughtered by the masses, is the perceived sense of intimate power. Your own voice, your capacity to command, is subjectively taken. However, you find that this is not so, and your injunctions upon the malicious acts do not go unheard. In fact, you are not only able to speak, but you mandate the cavern of fallacious ones to dissolve. Others can only take from you what you have been conditioned to believe is contingent upon physical acquirement. Once we have embraced these realities, we begin preparing to fully lose ourselves.

The human condition is both an idiosyncratic and universal plane. As we journey along the continuum, we observe and witness the many events and experiences which transcribe our own versions of humanness. These encounters concurrently are the infrastructure for communal humanness. Only once the realities of Yourself and Others unify to become Us, can an individual truly know the human condition.

Our common ground, shall only be found in the notion of our humanness. Following the solidifying process of our own existence, our own sphere, comes the presence of another reality, another sphere.

Here you find yourself in the divine interaction between you and others, eventually culminating in your final test of the disparate reality. Therefore, the experiences of Them becomes understood as fittingly titled, *Invocations*.

Them. *Invocations*

Division is a toxic beast, it is a grave distortion. What are the fruits of division? Throughout time, there is not one instance when a world divided thrived. Systematic, social, or cultural walls have never brought prosperity. The reality of 'Them' is a notion that has manifested the seeds of division since the dawn of human culture. Xenophobia is bred by ignorance and the belief structure that foreigners, or others in any regard, are not to be revered but feared. This system results in nothing but a world divided, either physically or institutionally. In a globalized society, we have the obligation to treat and experience all peoples, as not only our neighbors, but as an extension of ourselves.

Immediately following the absolution and dismantling of the guillotine, we find ourself before a terrifying entity. The demon, a creation of our own hands, stands between us and eventual communal solidarity. Not only does this demon suggest that we have pinpoints in our own pasts which prevent our ability to deconstruct walls we have built, but it also comments on the dangerous reality that even once we have assumed control of our autonomy, doubt can linger. Until we overcome the festering perversions of self-doubt, we have no hope of a lasting strength. Once the demon is demolished, we are accompanied by the presence of three old friends.

Into the clearing, the figures from our prior wandering make themselves known. The woman, those who deny that realities have passed through the barriers of time, presents herself. She cries, for she has learned that to search for unobtainable realities is unproductive, it is harmful, and constrains her to stagnation. A denier can never know full goodness, unparalleled enlightenment, they will always remain in a state of darkness. The man, those who search in the wrong places, for answers right before their eyes, reveals himself. He cries for he has found that righteousness for the sake of righteousness is not conducive to true inquiry. He has witnessed that following systems that are not intersectional, do not build upon the quality of diverse experience and shall never translate authentic humanness. The child, those who are locked in the unforgiving inertia of neglect and disillusionment. The ones who have been left, forsaken to stumble without guidance and love, the forgotten ones. They rejoice, for they have found the security and comfort they have never known. This triad of unfortunate souls have the answers they seek, by unshackling their bonds and journeying themselves.

The physical laying of objects forged by overcoming the most difficult aspects of ourselves upon the ground, signifies the transition from the first reality to the second. Once you have dissected yourself to the core, rooting out the totality of obstacles preventing unblemished solidarity, altruism can begin to form.

Within the clearing, a powerful phenomenon begins to take shape - the bedrock of human solidarity. Mirroring the masses who resided beneath the guillotine, the events in the clearing are the quintessence antithetical of empty solidarity. From among the vast forest pour hundreds of souls. Some of these individuals have been accompanying you along your trek, while others are fresh faces unseen before. Regardless of their origin in your passage, they celebrate in a communal resplendence for the elimination of their own demons. A potential for gatherings where all people are not only welcomed, but collectively celebrating shedding bondage, is the cornerstone of intersectionality. Without a knowledge and an active usage of intersectionality in all endeavors, true goodness becomes fruitless. The wisdom which comes from fusing intersectionality with individuality is a practice pivotal to the assurance of lasting solidarity.

Intersectionality is a heightened awareness of one's own experiences in conjunction with others, as well as other's experience with your own. It is a transaction and transcription of the relationship between two entities and their own distinct realities. The relations we hold as humans between our own aspects of identity, our associations with other communities and ideologies, and the ways in which social institutions affect us are intersectional. The bindings between complexities of the human condition are interconnected, they are as multiplex as the beings they transcend. We are infinite in our capacity for identity, for growth; in essence, we ourselves are Voids of our own design.

In this space among the trees, where goodness incarnate is conceived, you are lovingly guided by two figures. The first is an entity who has purposely been with you throughout the majority of the Void, a younger you. By watching you experience the tribulations and triumphs, they are learning the strength to one day surmount the very same trials. The second individual is also purposely placed in your pathway. The person is a woman, the very same who was mutilated by the guardians of the guillotine before you. In our current social climate, it would be remissful to have the soul who leads you into solidarity's sacred space be anyone but a woman of color. In a validation of intersectionality, she is also a disciple to a prophet of foreign origin to the masses. Her abuse, and seemingly silent acceptance of such treatment, is not meant to suggest she is not a person of powerful agency. In fact, the truth is quite the opposite. She is the beacon onward, the figurehead of forward progress through the Void. By witnessing her, you were compelled to continue. You listened to the oppressed and made the decision to follow her. As a collective family, we must listen, follow, and value the struggles of those facing oppression in order to build a venerating social order.

Once you have been brought into the forming circle, the ceremony of solidarity commences. From each hand, a candle is brought forth. Unlit and simple, the sticks of wax represent the human vessel - they are the reflection of the very beings who hold them. Upon speaking one's name, the orb, which manifested from the remnants of physically celebrating solidarity, bends and shares a sliver of illumination unto each wick. The power of a name, the very essence of each individual's personhood, is actualized through their recitation.

As the circle finds fulfillment, the orb depicts past possibilities, merging with the realities of future possibility. You are suggested not to dwell in the past, but to acknowledge its shortcomings. To embrace what has occurred, but to know that solidarity going onward shall build what could have been already. Until you have spoken your own truth, your own name, the sphere is unjoined and solidarity is not possible. When solidifying the circle with the addition of your name, the ceremony transitions from laying the foundation of solidarity to erecting it.

All peoples present break off, venturing into the surrounding space to acquire their sacred symbol. The embodiment of their own Voids - whether they are following in the footsteps of a religious leader, scientific inquiry, or introspective instruction. You find the symbol which perfectly manifests your own truths, and return to the clearing. As a collective entity, your grouping proceeds to lay the images upon a mighty heap in the center.

Only once the pile of personhoods has reached completion, can the gathering become one. With each individual laying their personhood down, shedding the vessel which bars them from stepping into full solidarity, full goodness, the circle becomes unrestricted to unify at center. At that moment, as all gathered stand together and step forward, you become one - one body, one goodness. The production of one goodness gives us a second spherical diagram to represent absolutes within the Void.

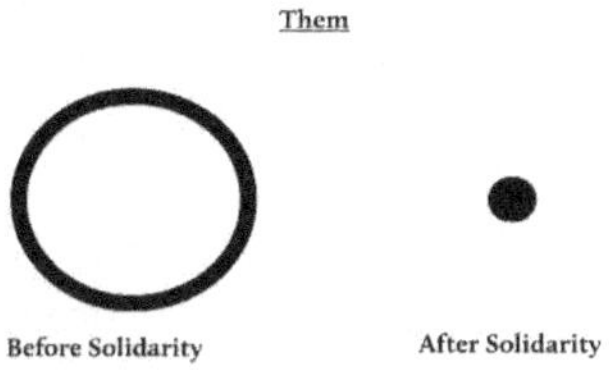

*for clarity, the diagrams are presented as circles.

Take notice of how when the completed sphere of 'You' is overlaid on the sphere of 'Them', the product is a thickened sphere. As intersectionality grows, so too does the potential for goodness to form. It is the engagement and invocation of intersectionality that gifts us the ability to formulate a pathway toward goodness. We know that to live an intersectional life, opens our souls and personhoods to join in a powerful union. Such a divine union is represented in the second sphere above.

When intersectionality collapses inward, and there is no distinction between one or another, human solidarity manifests. The Void's complete absolute is this truth. When we stand amongst one another, and shed our vessel of flesh, transcending the material, we are left with nothing but space to grow. Each time we reach this state, we are allowed unrestricted means by which to build. It is an ever-continuing process, the journey to the clearing. We must perpetually venture into ourselves, evaluate each instance of existence, every moment of breath, and map out our relations between ourselves and those around us.

Eventually, if all have walked the path, the world will be left with all peoples living an unrestricted sense of self and others. The palpable energy of intersectionality will bind us into an unending era of solidarity. The instant unblemished, communal solidarity transpires, a gorgeous binding of personhoods produces the incarnation of goodness - of true divinity. The creation and fallout of this supernova, Fragor Maximus, divine fusion gives way for the third, and final reality to be actualized. Within this reality, the fruits of uniting 'You' and 'Them' are evident through encompassing, ancient ideologies.

Us. *Final Venerations*

The existence of a universal divinity has been debated since the formation of human social structures. We have waged wars, built nations, and adhered to philosophical and moral paradigms rooted in the very concept of these proposed truths. They are the beliefs and ideologies that are argued to be existent outside the human vessel. They occur on a plane distinct from our own. Once we have found ourselves fused with the fruits of human solidarity, the notions of human spirituality become the byproduct.

Spirituality in this regard refers to the suggestion that there are realities that bind us which are outside our own bodies. The human spirit, the entity that is human solidarity, is synonymous with spirituality. For this reason, once human solidarity has been fulfilled, you are delivered to a space far above the ground. While you remain in the Void, you are in a place where the happenings below are examined from a seemingly separate plane.

Many names have been given to the entity you meet upon the boulder, to their energy, and the domain that they represent. They are the epitome of evil, the greatest sinner, one who committed highest crimes against human development. But what if they are just like us? They too were searching. They are not evil, but empty. When the notions of evilness are stripped from our vocabulary, and instead replaced with emptiness, we are left with a completely new understanding for the antithesis of goodness.

Emptiness has room for growth, for eventual fulfillment, for lasting goodness. If there is an individual, whether metaphorical or physical, who can be attributed all the 'evilness' in our world, we lose our need for agency. It is not the choices we make, but the presence of evil which creates barriers to goodness. It is not our own deficiencies of enacting goodness, but the reality that one is among us, preventing our potential for solidarity. In this way, we relinquish control of our personhood to the emptiness we find ourselves comfortable within, we become stagnate, and in turn, do not fulfill our goodness - our purpose. It is the mark of emptiness to believe inertia is progress, to find comfort only in the familiar and not upon the pathway of intersectional goodness. Once you have been made aware of who you speak with, their comrade - the embodiment of goodness fulfilled, living in authentic oneness - makes themselves known.

Before you materializes the figure who has been pursued throughout human history. They are the individual who manifests pure goodness, the reflection of divine order only found in human solidarity. By their speaking with you, and subsequent musical composition, you are gifted a glimpse into the pain they have witnessed. For past, present, and future eternities they had to watch as humanity consumed humanity. They held witness to every atrocity ever committed, even those which have yet to transpire. It must be understood that goodness carries the continued burden of bearing witness to the horrendous acts occurring around them. Goodness is not a state of bliss, but of awareness.

The weight of awareness is both the greatest gift of goodness while being the most anguishing attribute it bestows. Living in a constant state of goodness, we are plagued with the painful realities which tarnish our past, mark our present, and prevent a prosperous future. It is for this reason that obtaining goodness leads us to the divine knowledge that goodness is not complacent, is not comfortable.

We must continue to journey back into the Void. Witness, experience, and learn, each time visiting our introspective bedrock - the garden. Within those gates we add to our holy books, the pages transcribing our life voyage. This binding is what builds our personal souls, until we fade to mere memory, and our collection is placed in the halls of a cosmic library. The place where human goodness and solidarity reign, until the world here reflects such a reality.

Following the transcription of this Void, the figures of goodness and emptiness depart. You are left to spend a few moments discerning the trials and triumphs of this Void. Laid beneath you is the totality of your journey through this Void. In this moment, you have the privilege to find peace with this specific pilgrimage, while the obligation to acknowledge there are many more Voids to trek, far more work to be done. Concluding this Void, you are brought back to a familiar space. A small coffeehouse, metaphorically understood as the place of relief, the promised land. The young child with their guardians, hurried movement beyond the windows, the individual who serves your drink, they all hold an essence, a personhood. As you have come to know, the enlightened ones forevermore view the world through the lens of the Void and recognize the presence of other Voids all around them. Until the sphere concaves, and all are one, this is the pathway toward goodness.

The final diagrams, give us a most peculiar entity to understand. The complete union of all three realities, Cremations (You), Invocations (Them), and Final Venerations (Us), produces an arguably simple symbol. A single sphere, rotating around a center sphere of concrete presence is the communion of the triad. While this is the encompassing depiction of the Void, many may recognize a dually palpable representation below. Early philosophers called the image set here, the Monad, or the Greek word for "unit". The Monad is the iconic translation of the concept of The Absolute. The Void.

Us

*for clarity, the diagram is presented as a circle.

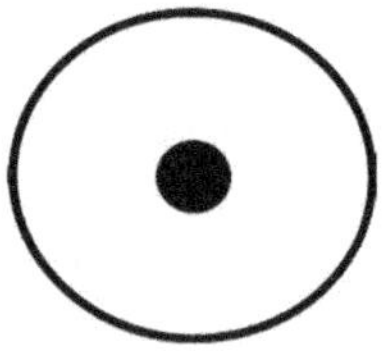

Through the diagrammatic representation for the trinity of realities, we are presented with the ancient ideology of The Absolute. As in the Void, when the limitless nature of the final reality forms, we are left with the unrestricted capacity to create. We are able to construct universes built upon the unshaken beliefs of goodness rooted in human solidarity, in oneness. When we become one, we are not only reflecting the absolute of divine goodness, but we quite literally become it. When we mirror the most intricate complexities of goodness, we are goodness.

We began with the unjoined sphere of our own selves. Willing to strike the match, daring to investigate our own minds, our essence and journey ourselves. Once we were stripped of ourselves, both by our own accord and the unforgiving degradation of the masses, we find our most valuable aspect of being. We can only lose what we allow to be taken. Yet, when we freely lay our personhood down, we are able to step into intersectional and solidarity prepared spaces - fulfilling our sphere and potential for goodness.

Once ready to meet the second reality we were brought forth from the confines of the first reality. The dual presences of You and Them unified, consummated a thickened sphere, nurtured by intersectionality and communal vulnerability. This sphere is the one which is bound by intersectional introspection and eventual solidarity. At the moment solidarity is actualized, the sphere solidifies, for solidarity is the closest binding.

The last reality envelopes the representation of solidarity, encompassing all that is Us. This is the reality which gives order to chaos and chaos to order. Within this furthest and final existence, we exist in nothing but solidarity. We are many, but one. We are contained, yet limitless. We are bound to one another, but freedom of essence is finally realized.

When one dissects the construction of The Absolute - The Void - they will find numerous properties of powerful meaning. Below, the complete fulfillment of the Void is shown, with a number of line segments branching from the center. These lines illustrate the geometric absolute of the Void. No matter where one plots a length from center to the outer sphere, the distance is equal in all instances. In this way, one can assert that any argument which

<u>Us</u>

*for clarity, the diagram is presented as a circle.

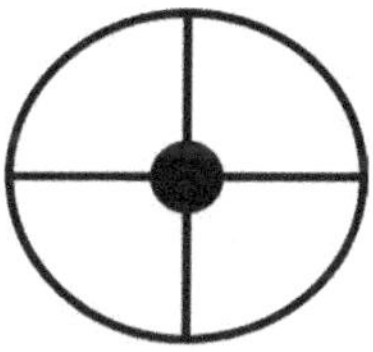

is rooted in the Void's symmetrical absolute is equal in measure to all other arguments. It does not matter what you deem the title of the Void experience. The pathway to goodness can be a faith, a religion, a philosophy, a science, an art, or none of these. What the Void is seen as to one, does not need to translate to another, for the Void is an absolute that is not founded on a singular translation. It does not lose any potency or truth when interpreted differently, for it is the absolute. Due to this phenomenon, we can quantify the realities of the Void as an endless spectrum of explanations for the Void itself and all things which exist within and without its presence. The attributions are subjective for the individual experiences are solely those of the traveler.

This work is not an attempt at proposing a novel religious dogma. The ideologies of 'spirituality' are set in the context of amplifying the notion that there is a greater presence outside our own autonomous bodies, i.e. human solidarity. In order to adequately transcend the world's material constructs, it was only appropriate for the journey to occur on a plane that both mirrored the material, and existed apart from such constructs.

This work is also not a supportive argument for relativism's philosophical proponents. While relativism plays a role in the unique and idiosyncratic aspects of each wayfarer's experience in the Void, the Void is an absolute. Therefore, these assertions cannot be relative in totality, as there is an absolute where they all stem. The Void, the very journey of the human narrative, is undeniably understood as one organic experience when all are traveling a radius toward goodness.

It is our burden, our most defining experience as human beings, to journey the Void. To bind ourselves with one another and hold the pain we experience as one. We must be there together in triumphs and resolute during tragedies. We cannot negate the dignity of one and sanctify the worth of another - this merely erases any form of true validation. We have been given the roadway to goodness, but to fully enact it, we must venture ourselves, those around us, and manifest these experiences as a paradigm for our future.

The future forward shall also be one of our own design. We are the curators of culture, the creators of history, and the pedagogues of forthcoming generations. Our mark is one of great significance, as was those before us. We must be a people defined by our amplification of the Void and its realities. We must strive to be a communal voice, one which values all who exist, no matter their personhood.A society which promotes any moral compass apart from goodness, true solidarity in human form, does nothing but contribute to the continued existence of the cloth. We must not be such a society. It will be difficult. It is difficult. There will be times when it feels we are nourishing goodness on our own, that we have been left to tend a flame with no comfort from another's presence. Yet, we must not forget that even a solitary presence of goodness, means that goodness is present in the world. Be that goodness. Light the flame and continue to beacon others onward, into the Void and toward solidarity. Toward goodness.

....

It was during the seasonal metamorphosis of Winter to Spring in 2016 that I began writing this collection. Initially I wanted to craft a work that centered on the individual healing of a single person over their tribulations. Throughout my preliminary drafts and production, I began to find myself unable to break from reality to enter into a state where literary art took precedence. Along with the global community, I was observing the unfolding of a presidential election in the United States. The desire to outline an immersive experience of healing, the road to authentic goodness, and the foundations of a passionately compassionate world, drove me to reevaluate my original plans. Thus, *This Void Beckons* transitioned from a manuscript following the healing of one individual, to a proposal for redeeming the human narrative.

In order to analyze the most intricate aspects of the human condition, I began to ponder on what binds us. Where I found myself was a most unpredicted place - the religious dogma I was raised within. In the Roman Catholic Church, it is understood that Jesus Christ sacrificed his life for the redemption of the world. It is this driving belief which cultivates the foundation of Christian faith. However, as I grew to learn, believing in a paradigm that has been absolutely fulfilled breeds issues with complacency. If divine goodness has been achieved, then all one must do is reap the rewards from such a grace and exist with the knowledge that their contributions across the spectrum of action are forgivable. There is no need to walk the way, if it has been surmounted. It was in this moment of realization where I began to journey my own Void.

As a queer person, more specifically a transgender individual, I have always been accustomed to finding myself in spaces where I felt I was not valued. It was not until I began to work in solidarity movements and community engagement atmospheres that I tasted what true veneration was. Concurrent with experiencing validation, I was a witness to the oppression and treatment of those around me. This dual existence is a disillusioning experience. I found myself feeling my actualized solidarity only put an extremely small dent in the mountain of oppression. I came to realize that in order to uproot oppression, actively combat it, and cultivate lasting solidarity - there needed to be a bridge between all sides of any issue. In that moment, the literary construction of an indisputable, absolute journey began to be transcribed.

As the Void began to fully form, I was taken into places I had never even conceptualized in the beginning. It became apparent to me that, when writing this work, I needed to give readers a deeply intimate experience of the Void. For the work to have any potential impact, I needed to dismantle a major tenant of art - the fourth wall. The experiences of the Void, having been undeniably laid out as universal, yet interpersonal, could only be narrated effectively if the narrative was speaking directly to the reader.

The reader needed to feel the heartache, not just because there was heartache, but because it was their own. The reader needed to experience their tongue being taken from them, but not just the tongue of a character in the book - their own tongue. The reader must believe this is their story, not only because it must be for palpable change to occur in the world, but because this is their story. The narrative of the Void is the human condition. It is the human narrative. This is our legacy, and it resides in spaces within each of us. To tap into that space and invite the greater populous of readership to journey these aspects of themselves, truly investigating who they are and what their purpose is, was the reason this manuscript could not have a fourth wall.

While in the midst of drafting this work, I continually journeyed back to that initial place where I had found myself pondering what binds the human family. Though I am fully aware it would be quite misinformed to assert that all human solidarity hinges on the Christian faith, I did find myself digesting the right information. Eventually, I would come to realize the reasoning for my deeper examining of faith and religion.

This work, the notion of the Void, and its application to various schools of thought, has less to do with my own finding of the path as it has to do with the path itself. The reason one can stumble upon the Void if they have experienced a religious background is solely due to the message. These prophets, thinkers, leaders, and visionaries all have one thing in common - their work is unfinished. They were all leading us to the Void, to this pattern and order of how to adequately build a better future. We must follow the path that has been walked for millennia, in order to not only fulfill the work which has been started by hundreds, but complete our own contributions to this gorgeous narrative.

Now, what may feel like the most arduous question before us is where do we go from here. We have journeyed the Void. We have witnessed. We have learned. We have gazed upon the divinity that is solidarity. We have acquired the paradigm of universal knowledge. Is there hope? Is there the possibility of human redemption? Of perpetual peace? Therein lies the beauty of the human narrative. Simply understand, yes, there is hope. Human redemption can be on the horizon. It must be. We can not afford it to be a fantasy any longer. We must build this reality. A narrative where the unification of You and Them to produce US is actualized. This is our duty. Our eternal dance. Our purpose. Our cosmic Void.

I firmly believe in this work. I believe the bedrock of the collective human soul is one of goodness. The potential for human greatness is undeniably before us. We must be resolute on our campaign toward greatness of character, value, dignity, and goodness. We must not hold hate for any soul, any community, any 'sinner'. Do not even entertain hatred in any form. Holding hatred shall only leave us closer to emptiness than the divinity of goodness. A clenched fist can never hold the hand of its neighbor. It can never build what could be, but only destroys what is.

It is our greatest prayer as a human family. To shed hatred, emptiness, and ignorance in all forms in our journey onward. Together, we can surmount the terrifyingly gorgeous incline of human possibility. Let us go on. Let us continue the journey of the Void.

I bid you well, my dearest companion. I invoke nothing but warmth, wisdom, and fruition in all endeavors unto you. Until the pages bring us together once more, selfishly acquire the goodness we so desperately need, and selflessly share it with each soul you encounter. Till the sphere collapses inward, may we begin again.

The world. The journey. The Void. Await.

Most Sincerely in Ink,

a. j. k. o'donnell

| *Acknowledgements*

This work is not one solely of my own experiences. Countless individuals have journeyed the way while I did. They helped me in the darkness and they gave me clarity when I faltered. I would be committing a horrendous misdeed if I did not extend my sincerest gratitude to them.

Kristi Tackett-Newburg for continually giving me unfailing, unconditional love. I found a home with you. Ben, Aly, and Emy, you gave me a laugh and warmth I had forgotten where to find.

Jim Rogers of the Colin Higgins Foundation and Claire Dietz at the Daily Iowan for taking the time to read and provide initial reviews for this work. Your patience and support as the manuscript finalized was much appreciated.

My editors Emily Hough and Alec McMullen for their love of the written and aid in sculpting this work to its most artisically, articulate form. Your presence and heartfelt suggestions are always a blessing.

My Caffeine Dreams family for more than half a decade of serenity. While this is the final work I conduct from beginning to end within these walls, I will forever call this place my primary residence. It is where my soul found itself, and for all those who were a part of that experience, I say an immense thank you.

Dearest friends and family, comrades and strangers of Omaha, Nebraska, the city which birthed me. As I move on in this life, I will always return home to coldest of winters and warmest of nights. After living in almost every corner of our city, I have come to know so many of you. Educators who believed in me. Dear friends who sat with me in exposed brick coffeehouses. Loved ones who traveled to distant cities, exploring reservoirs and awing California skylines from the Chateau Marmont. My family for being on this journey with me. The earliest supporters to the earliest critiques, I am grateful for all you have shared with me.

Finally, to you. For taking the time and emotional energy to read this manuscript. I deeply hope it brings you closer on your own journey toward goodness.

| *a.j.k. o'donnell*

andrew joseph kimberley o'donnell is an acclaimed American author, poet, and award-winning activist. Born in Omaha, Nebraska in 1997, she began writing works before the age of eight. She is the author of the collection *Nicoteane and Other Foolish Mistakes,* the short story *Confessions of a Fearful Soul,* and the narrative collection *This Void Beckons.*

She was a 2016 recipient of the prestigious Youth Courage Award, presented by the *Colin Higgins Foundation*, honored as an Outstanding Young Omaha Teen in 2015, and the 2014 Maha Poetry Festival Champion. In 2017, she was a contributing writer with the *Huffington Post,* penning the ongoing series, *A Life in Transitions.*

When she is not writing, which is quite the rare occasion indeed, she can be found at familiar, cozy coffeehouses, walking in parks near her home, and watching cars drive by from her apartment windowsill. Her third work and debut novel, *What the Crevice Holds,* is forthcoming from Cracked Jar Press.

She currently resides in the Midwest, where she is pursuing a BA.

Further information regarding o'donnell can be found on **www.ajkodonnell.com**

Instagram: ajkodonnell

Twitter: @ajkodonnell

Facebook: AJK O'Donnell

| o'donnell in 2016 |

Courtesy of Joshua Foo Photography

to begin again

until oblivion

claims us

www.ingramcontent.com/pod-product-compliance
Lightning Source LLC
Chambersburg PA
CBHW022101090426
42743CB00008B/680
9780997767001